Natural

Business Startup

How to Start, Run & Grow a Profitable Beef Jerky Business From Home!

By

Jim Davis

WHAT'S INSIDE

INTRO TO JERKY

In this book, I'm going to take you through the process of making natural jerky and turning it into a business that takes advantage of this rising demand for all natural jerky meat products. I'll discuss the sources of meat and how to choose the best ones as well as the various processes used to make jerky and process meat. We'll discuss the hygiene requirements for jerky processing. Then we'll look at how you can start your business and make it successful. In the end, I'll include a few awesome jerky recipes to help you get started.

But first, let's start from the very beginning.

Statistics show that meat consumption in developing countries has steadily increased from 22 lbs. per capita in the 1960s to 57 lbs. per capita in 2000. It is estimated that this will increase to about 85 lbs. per capita by 2030. In developed countries, the rate of meat consumption is at a stagnant high level.

In developing countries, the increase in demand for meat is often the result of urbanization where city residents tend to spend more for food than the rural residents. Often as soon as a consumer can afford it, they tend to lean more towards animal protein, meat in particular, in their daily diet. Even as meatless diets become popular, the majority of individuals will continue to eat meat since it is often accepted that a balanced diet for human needs both meat and plant food.

From a nutritional standpoint, meat and other animal derived foods are high sources of protein than plant foods. Meat also contains the essential amino acids which are the integral organic components of protein that can't be made in the human organism. Animal protein is also the only source of Vitamin B12. Meat is also rich in iron, making it important for preventing anemia in pregnant women and children.

When it comes to meat production, the trend is clear, annual production in 2006 was 267 million, and by 2016 it was 320 million. Developing countries account for over 50 million of this. However, to meet the rising demand for meat; alternatives need to be found for making better use of meat resources and reducing the waste of edible livestock parts.

This is why meat processing is so important. It completely uses meat resources, including nearly all edible parts for human consumption. Meat processing involves the manufacture of meat products from muscle, fat and certain non-meat additives. The additives are there to help enhance flavor and appearance.

Processing meat into jerky offer economic, dietary and sensory benefits that you don't get from fresh meat. Let's consider some of the benefits that come from jerky meat:

1. All edible parts of the animal that are suitable for processing can be used.

2. Lean meat is the most valuable but is also the highest in cost; making it less affordable for certain populations. Jerky combines lean meat with other products, creating a low-cost product that more consumers can afford to buy and have access to

animal protein. This is also important for women and children in low-income groups, who can benefit from the amino acids, vitamins, and minerals in meat products.

3. Processed meat like jerky can also be made shelf stable, unlike fresh meat. This means that they can be kept without refrigeration in one of three ways: as heat sterilized canned products, as fermented and slightly dried products or as dried jerky forms, where bacterial growth is inhibited.

These meats are easy to store and transport without refrigeration to areas that don't have cold storing facilities.

4. Processing meat such ways can also add value to the product. This is through a unique flavor, taste, color or texture that you won't get from fresh meat. This makes jerky more diverse, allowing people to experiment and find a unique combination of nutritious food and taste.

Let us take a brief moment to consider the history and diversity of meat processing technology.

HISTORY AND DIVERSITY OF MEAT PROCESSING TECHNOLOGY

Most meat processing technologies were developed in Europe and Asia. Obviously, European technologies were more successful; becoming more disseminated and adopted by other regions throughout the world. European technologies focused on burger patties, frankfurter-type sausages, and cooked hams. Most Asian types focused on fermented meats that are still popular in their various countries of origin. In recent years, Western-style products have become increasingly popular and have achieved a higher market share.

In some Asian and African countries meat is very popular, but most consumers reject processed meat for socio-cultural reasons that prevent them from consuming certain livestock species; often beef or pork. However, with the demand for meat increasing and more processing leading to single source animal products such as jerky; more consumers are now adjusting and enjoying the benefits of processed meats.

So let's begin by taking a look at meat in general and what makes a good meat choice for jerky making.

MEAT SOURCES

Meat, fat and other carcass parts are used as raw materials to make a variety of meat products and jerky in particular. Most jerky meat come from domesticated animal species such as cows, pigs, and poultry; but some jerky makers do choose to use buffalo, sheep and goat meat. In some regions, it is also popular to use camels, jaks, horses and game animals (though I never have).

When it comes to jerky, the term meat is often defined as the muscle tissue of slaughtered animals. However, the other important issue when it comes to jerky is fat. Often the other edible parts such as the internal organs and by-products such as blood, aren't used in the jerky making process. However, if you choose to do a complete process of your slaughtered animal, you can use these other parts to create other processed meat such as sausages.

It is vital to note the importance of the intestines in meat processing. In many regions, it is used as food, but they can also be processed in a way to make sausage casings. Some are processed to be eaten with the sausage while others are peeled off before eating. Although that is entirely a different topic that we won't get into within the scope of this book but maybe I will writer another entire book on sausage making process in the near future.

Occasionally, the skin of some species will be used to make processed meat products. This is often only the case with pork skin, poultry skin and in a few instances calfskin. I don't want to get too technical in this book, but let's at least take a moment to look at the chemical aspects of meat composition to better understand how to handle it during the jerky making process.

MUSCLE MEAT

Meat is generally composed of water, fat, protein, minerals and little bit of carbohydrate. As you likely gathered from the introduction, the most important nutritional component of meat is the protein. The protein contents and values are what determines the quality of the raw meat material and its suitability for further processing into jerky. Consider the following table to help you understand the chemical makeup of various types of meat in comparison with some common types of food.

Food	Water	Protein	Fat	Ash	Calories/100g
Lean Beef	75.0	22.3	1.8	1.2	116
Beef Carcass	54.7	16.5	28.0	0.8	323
Lean Pork	75.1	22.8	1.2	1.0	112
Pork Carcass	41.1	11.2	47.0	0.6	472

Lean Veal	76.4	21.3	0.8	1.2	98
Chicken	75.0	22.8	0.9	1.2	105
Venison	75.7	21.4	1.3	1.2	103
Beef Fat	4.0	1.5	94.0	0.1	854
Pork Fat	7.7	2.9	88.7	0.7	812
Fried Lean Beef	58.4	30.4	9.2		213
Fried Lean Pork	59.0	27.0	13.0		233

Fried Lean Lamb	60.9	28.5	9.5		207
Fried Lean Veal	61.7	31.4	5.6		186
Ham Sausage	68.5	16.4	11.1		170
Raw Cooked Sausage	57.4	13.3	22.8	3.7	277
Frankfurter	63.0	14.0	19.8	0.3	240
Liver Sausage	45.8	12.1	38.1		395

e					
Liver Pate	53.9	16.2	25.6	1.8	307
Gelatinous Meat Mix	72.9	18.0	3.7		110
Salami	33.9	24.8	37.5		444
Pasteurized Milk	87.6	3.2	3.5		63
Boiled Egg	74.6	12.1	11.2		158
Rye Bread	38.5	6.4	1.0		239

Cooked Potatoes	78.0	1.9	0.1		72

What this table shows is that the water is a variable in all the components and it is often closely and inversely linked to the fat content. This is why the fat content is higher in whole carcasses than a lean cut. The fat content is also higher in processed meat products that use a large amount of fatty tissue.

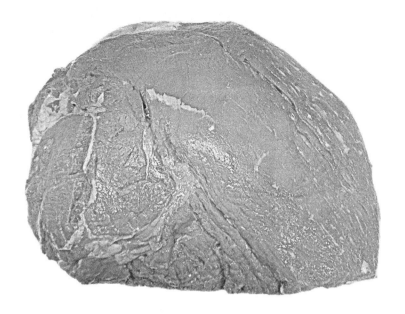

As I've already said, the value of animal foods is essential in the content of proteins. Protein is comprised of 20 amino acids. Nearly 65% of the proteins in an animal are skeleton muscle protein, 30% are connective tissues proteins, and 5% are blood proteins and keratin or hairs and nails.

STRUCTURE OF MUSCLE TISSUE

Muscles are surrounded by connective tissue membrane. The ends of this membrane meet and merge into a tendon that attaches to the skeleton. Individual muscles contain several muscle fiber bundles that can be seen by the naked eye. These bundles contain a range of 30 to 80 muscle fibers or muscle cells. They are a few centimeters long and are about 0.01 to 0.1 mm in diameter. The size and diameter of muscle fibers depend on the age, type, and breed of the animal. In between these bundles, there are blood vessels along with connective tissue and fat deposits. Each muscle cell is surrounded by a cell membrane known as sarcolemma. Inside the cell are sarcoplasma and a number of filaments known as myofibrils

The sarcoplasma is a soft protein structure that contains the red muscle pigment called myoglobin. Myoglobin is responsible for absorbing the oxygen carried by small blood vessels and stores the oxygen reserve for contracting the living muscle. The myoglobin in meat is responsible for providing the red meat color and plays a major part in the curing reaction.

The sarcoplasma makes up about 30% of the muscle cell. Sarcoplasmic proteins are water soluble. Nearly 70% of muscle cells are made up of myofibrils, which are a solid protein chain with a diameter or 0.001 to 0.002 mm. These proteins are what make up the significant nutritional value of muscle cell proteins and are soluble in a saline solution. This is important information in the production of certain meat products, but most specifically raw-cooked products and cured-cooked products. This is because of the heat coagulation of the liquefied myofibril proteins in these processes. The coagulated proteins are what provides the typical solid-elastic texture in the final jerky products.

Another important thing to consider in the chemical makeup of meat is the pH and the changes it undergoes since it has an impact on the taste, flavor and storage life of meat.

MEAT AND PH

Immediately after slaughter, animal muscle contains a small amount of a particular carbohydrate known as glycogen. Most of this is broken down into lactic acid within the first hours after slaughtering. This biochemical process is important in the function of establishing acidity or low pH of meat.

This glycolytic cycle starts at slaughter when the glycogen is broken down into lactic acid. As lactic acid builds up in the muscle and causes an increase in acidity, which is measured by pH. The pH of a normal muscle at the time of slaughter is about 7.0, but it quickly decreases in meat. In a typical animal, about 24 hours after slaughter the ultimate pH falls to about 5.8 to 5.4. This degree of reduction after slaughter has a great effect on the quality of the meat.

The ideal taste and flavor of the meat are only achieved once the pH drops down to 5.8 to 5.4. When it comes to processing meat, those with a pH of 5.6 to 6.0 is best for products needing water binding such as frankfurters and cooked ham. For products that lose water during processing and ripening such as dry sausages and jerky; meat with a pH around 5.6 to 6.2 is better since it has a lower water binding capacity.

pH also plays a major role in the storage life of meat. The lower the pH, the less likely bacterial growth is to occur. If animals have depleted their glycogen reserves before slaughtering, they won't have a sufficient drop in pH and are highly prone to bacterial deterioration. This is typical of animals that undergo stressful transportation or handling in holding pens before slaughter and processing.

In animals, under stress, the pH can quickly fall to 5.8 to 5.6 while the carcass is still warm. This is often seen in pork. It is seen as meat with a pale color and a soft, nearly mushy texture with a wet surface. This type of meat will have lower binding properties and loses weight rapidly during the jerky making process that results in a decreased processing yield.

The reverse can actually happen in animals that haven't been fed for a while before slaughter or those who are fatigued during transport. In these cases, most muscle glycogen is used up by slaughter, and the needed acidity doesn't occur in the meat. In these animals, the muscle pH often doesn't fall below 6.0. This meat is often seen as dark, firm and dry. This high pH causes the muscle proteins to retain their bound water. With these meats, less moisture loss occurs during the jerky making process. This improves the conditions for the growth of microorganisms; resulting in a shorter shelf life for the meat. These conditions can occur in both beef and pork products.

Both of these types of meat are still fit for human consumption but aren't ideal for cooking, frying or jerky making. However, for meat processing purposes you can still use these meats, but you should blend them with regular meat. This brings us to the discussion of the water holding capacity of meat.

WATER HOLDING CAPACITY OF MEAT

The water holding capacity of meat is an important factor in the quality of meat from both a consumer and processing point of view. Muscle proteins are able to hold a lot of water molecules on their surface. As muscle tissue develops acidity from a decrease of pH, the water holding ability decreases.

Water bound to the muscle protein affects the processing and eating quality of the meat. To get good yields during the processing of meat you often need a high water holding capacity. With the exception of jerky making where you need to lose water during processing.

Water holding capacity will vary based on the muscles in the animal and the species. Beef often has the greatest capacity for water retention and then pork with poultry having the least. Another aspect to consider is that of coloring.

MEAT COLORING

The characteristic color of meat is gained through a red pigment called myoglobin. This is similar to the blood pigment hemoglobin. It transports oxygen to the tissues of live animals.

Myoglobin is specifically the oxygen reserve for the muscle cells and fibers.

Oxygen is needed for the biochemical process that helps muscle contraction in animals. The higher the myoglobin concentration, the more intense the coloring of the muscle. The difference in myoglobin concentration is why one muscle group is lighter or darker in color than others within the same animal carcass.

The myoglobin concentration will also be different between various species. Beef often has more myoglobin than pork, veal or lamb and thus has a darker and more intense color. The pigment intensity is also influenced by the maturity of the animal. The levels of myoglobin will also determine how capable the meat is of curing. The red curing color of meat comes from the chemical reaction of myoglobin with the substance nitrite. Another area to consider is that of meat tenderness and flavor.

MEAT TENDERNESS AND FLAVOR

When an entire piece of meat is cooked, fried or barbecued; meat tenderness plays an essential role. Certain types of meat, beef, in particular, needs to undergo a ripening or aging period before it can be cooked and consumed in order to reach appropriate tenderness. When it comes to processed meat products, the toughness or tenderness is often of minor importance.

Most processed meats use comminuted meat, a process that causes even tough meat to become palatable. Additional processing of larger pieces of meat will result in a good chewing quality since they are often cured and fermented or cured and cooked which causes the meat to become more tender.

The taste of the meat will depend on the animal species. However, in certain food preparations, it can sometimes be difficult to determine the species. For example, in some ways, pork and veal may taste similar with the same chewing propertles.

Mutton and lamb have the same taste and smell as a result of the fat. Even a small amount of inter- and intramuscular fat can cause a typical smell and taste, especially meat from a more mature animal.

What an animal eats will also impact the taste of the meat. In addition, the sex of an animal can have an impact on the taste and smell of the meat. For example, boar's meat can have a pronounced urine-like smell.

The most desirable taste and odor of meat are often the results of the lactic acid formation. This occurs as a result of the glycogen breakdown within the muscle tissue. It can also be found in organic compounds such as amino acids and di- and tri-peptide proteins. Aged or mature meat often gets its characteristic taste from the breakdown of these substances. The "meaty" taste can be enhanced by the addition of monosodium glutamate (MSG). In some meat dishes, MSG is frequently used in Asian countries.

Lastly, you want to consider the impact of animal fats.

ANIMALS FATS

A natural occurring part of the animal carcass is fatty tissues. Within the live animal, fatty tissues serve three main functions:

1. Energy deposits and storage.

2. Insulation from body temperature loss.

3. Protective padding around organs such as the heart and kidneys.

Fatty tissue is made up of cells that, like other cells in the body, have cell membranes, nucleus, and matrix. The cell matrix is significantly reduced in order to provide additional space for fat storage. The fat that accumulates in cells comes from triglycerides. Animals that are well fed accumulate large amounts of fat within their tissues. The fat is gradually reduced from the fat cells during periods of starvation and/or exhaustion.

Animals also have subcutaneous fat deposits, fat deposits around the organs and inter-muscular fat or fat between the muscles. The fat between the muscle fibers is responsible for the higher accumulations of marbling. This marbling leads to tenderness and flavor that is unique to meats. For processed meats, fat is used to make the products softer while improving taste and flavor. In order to properly use animal fats, you need to have a basic understanding of fat selection and proper utilization.

Certain animal species have fat tissues that are better suited for meat products than other species. This is largely for the purpose of sensory experience since taste and flavor of fat will vary between species. There is also a sharp difference between older and younger animals. For example, older sheep have fat which is not suitable for use in processed meat.

Another factor involved in processing is the availability of fatty tissues. Some species have a higher amount of fatty tissue such as pigs, while others have less fat such as cows. Pig fat is popular in many regions for using in meat processing. Not only is pig fat easily available; but it also has a good tissue structure, composition, and unpronounced taste. Fresh pork fat is nearly odor and flavorless. Other animal fats with good processing potential have limited availability and/or undesirable taste.

PORK FAT

The subcutaneous fat found in pigs is the best suited and most widely used for meat processing. This is often found in back fat, jowl fat and the belly. These fatty tissues can easily be separated and used as an ingredient in processed meat products.

Sometimes the intermuscular fats in certain areas of the muscle tissue may be utilized. They are either trimmed from the muscle tissue or left connected and processed together. Both subcutaneous and intermuscular fats are known as body fats.

Another option is the depot fats or those found around internal organs. These fats can be separated before use. In pigs, most often the intestinal fats are used for softer meat products such as sausages. The kidney and leaf fat is often not used in processed meat products because of their hardness and taint, but they are frequently used in lard production.

BEEF FAT

Beef fat is often less suitable for processing than pork fat since it is firmer in texture, yellow in color and has a more intense flavor. When used for the purpose of processing, it is often the brisket fat and other body fats that are used from young animals. These fats are often used in processed beef products where pork fats need to be excluded for socio-cultural or religious purposes.

BUFFALO FAT

This fat has a whiter color than beef fat and is better suited for processing. The limiting factor is in its availability since buffalo carcasses don't have high quantities of body fats suitable for use in meat products.

GOAT/LAMB FAT

This fat from adult animals is often unsuitable for human consumption because of an unpleasant flavor. Lamb fat is often neutral in taste and eaten with lamb chops. Lamb fat is sometimes used as a fat source for Halal meat products.

CHICKEN FAT

This fat is neutral in taste and well suited for use in pure chicken products. Chicken fat often adheres to chicken muscle tissue as inter-muscle fat and needs to be processed without separating it from the meat. The majority of chicken fat comes from the skin. During processing, chicken skin is often minced and further processed into a fat emulsion before being added.

SELECTION AND GRADING OF MEAT

Any processed meat product is made up of animal muscle meat and animal fat. Muscle meat also contains some connective tissue and inter- and intramuscular fat that determine the quality of the meat. Animal fats are firm or soft in texture depending on the location within the animal. The texture of fat determines the processing quality of the meat.

The first step in processing meat is to selection raw meat, remembering to consider the quality and processing suitability of the meat along with the meat characteristics. Some species require you to have lean meat without adhering fat or connective tissues, while other species need a higher fat and/or connective tissue content to be successfully processed. Sometimes you'll need a firm animal fat, and others need soft fats. Choosing the right raw meat material for efficient beef jerky processing is done through a visual selection and grading based on the tissue specific properties.

If you are going to make beef jerky you want to develop your own specific standards of raw meat composition for your needs. This proper grading will be developed through skills and experience but will have a direct impact on the quality of the meat products you produce and the revenue you can get. To help you get started let's consider some general grading schemes for the basic meat such as pigs, cows/buffalo, ruminants, and poultry.

6 PIG MEAT SELECTION AND GRADING

When it comes to pig meat, common cuts used for fresh meat include the tenderloin, loin, rump, the entire ham and parts such as the topside, silverside, and knuckle along with parts of the neck and shoulder. Meat from pigs consists of six grades that can be refined or simplified based on consumer demand. The grades are as follows.

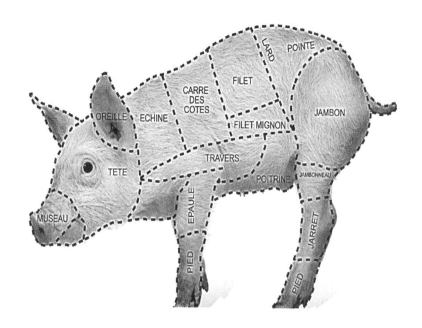

Grade 1 Pork - Lean muscle meat with all visible fat and connective tissues both hard and soft removed

This meat comes from body parts that have large muscle groups like the loin, hind leg, and shoulder. This meat is achieved during the preparation of choice cuts. Since more of this meat is needed for processing, some of the cuts can be used entirely to make jerky. Muscle groups that have a high connective tissue content such as the neck and thin shoulders aren't considered Grade 1 Pork meat.

Grade 2 Pork - Muscle meats with some solid fats embedded and connective tissue removed

This meat typically comes from the leaner parts of the pig such as the belly near the loin and pieces trimmed from the hind legs. The fat content of Grade 2 Pork meat shouldn't be over 25%. The embedded fatty tissue needs to be firm and dry since these cuts of meats typically aren't used for coarse meat products where fat particles are visible and sensed during chewing. This is why all visible hard and soft connective tissues need to be removed. This grade of pork meat is often reserved for use in sausages, lunch meat, and some reconstituted hams.

Grade 3 Pork - Muscle meat trimmings with low fat content, but larger amounts of soft connective tissue

This meat can come from all parts of the pig, but most manufacturers use the front quarter of the pig. Because of the smaller or larger amounts of soft connective tissues in these cuts they are often used for finely-chopped meat mixes. Often the hard connective tissue is removed, and the embedded fatty tissue of either a soft or firm texture isn't to exceed 10%.

Grade 4 Pork - Back fat

When manufacturers cut up a pork carcass, the fatty tissue is divided into soft and firm tissue. The firm and dry fat are considered Grade 4 Pork and exclusively comes from the fatty layer under the skin on the back. This back fat is often used for sausages or finely chopped meat mixed.

Grade 5 Pork - Soft fatty trimmings

Aside from the back fat that makes up Grade 4 Pork, there are other soft fatty tissues that are gained from a pork carcass. Since these trimmings have an oily and wet appearance, they are often considered unsuitable for making coarse products but can be mixed into finely chopped meat mix to make up the 25% fat portion needed.

Grade 6 Pork - Pork skin

Pork is one of the rare animal skins that is used as food as well as leather production. Since the pork skin is often exposed to contamination during slaughtering and cutting it is important to get pork skin that is of good hygienic quality. On the outside, pork skin should be free of hair and other impurities while on the inside all connected fatty tissue should be removed.

3 COW MEAT SELECTION AND GRADING

The choice cuts of cow meat are often used as fresh meat while the rest is used for further processing. Common fresh meat cuts that you find in grocery stores include tenderloin, sirloin, topside, silverside, rump and parts of the neck and shoulder. The rest of the cow is used for making processed meat products.

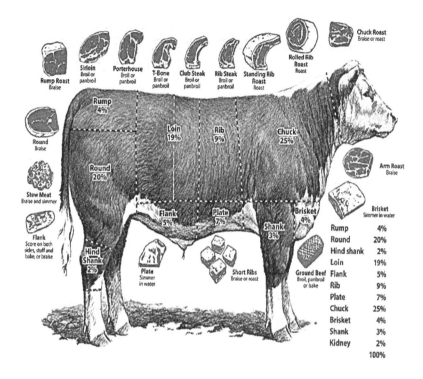

Chuck Roast
Braise or roast

Sirloin
Broil or panbroil

Porterhouse
Broil or panbroil

T-Bone
Broil or panbroil

Club Steak
Broil or panbroil

Rib Steak
Broil or panbroil

Standing Rib Roast
Roast

Rolled Rib Roast
Roast

Rump Roast
Braise

Round
Braise

Stew Meat
Braise and simmer

Flank
Score on both sides, stuff and bake, or braise

Rump 4%

Loin 19%

Rib 9%

Chuck 25%

Round 20%

Arm Roast
Braise

Flank 5%

Plate 7%

Shank 3%

Brisket 4%

Brisket
Simmer in water

Hind Shank 2%

Plate
Simmer in water

Short Ribs
Braise or roast

Ground Beef
Broil, panbroil or bake

Rump	4%
Round	20%
Hind shank	2%
Loin	19%
Flank	5%
Rib	9%
Plate	7%
Chuck	25%
Brisket	4%
Shank	3%
Kidney	2%
	100%

The functional properties of beef are largely influenced by the age of the animal. Young beef has a higher water binding capacity than meat from an older cow. This is why meat from younger animals is needed for products that rely on high binding and water holding capacity. Meat from older cows is better for products that require a drying and fermentation process.

Similar to the pork grading system, beef has a simple scheme to use for selecting and grading meat. However, beef only has three grades of meat since fat and skin are often not used for human consumption.

Grade 1 Beef - Lean muscle meat with all visible fat and connective tissue removed

This meat often comes from the major muscle groups of the fore and hindquarter of the cow with the exception of the belly muscles and shanks.

Grade 2 Beef - Muscle meat trimmings with small amounts of connective tissue and body fats under 10%

These meat parts are typically obtained from muscle trimmings of the prime meat cuts above and from smaller lean muscles that aren't used for the prime cuts.

Grade 3 Beef - Muscle meat trimmings with connective tissue and body fats under 20%

This grade of meat usually consists of meat trimmings removed during deboning or small trimmings from the flanks and shanks. Since this meat is often highest in connective tissue and/or fat, it is usually reserved for use in finely chopped meat mix. It is often tough in texture, which makes it unsuitable for use as coarse parts in meat mixes.

BUFFALO MEAT SELECTION AND GRADING

Buffalo meat is popular in some region such as Asia but is quickly becoming more popular in other parts of the world as well. The grading system for Buffalo is the same as that for cattle discussed above, but buffalo meat does have the right properties that make it great for further processing. Buffalo meat has a pronounced red color, good water binding capacity, and a unique flavor. Buffalo meat differs from beef in a few ways.

Color

Buffalo meat is slightly darker in color than beef. When processed, buffalo meat is darker and has a more intense red color than beef.

Taste

Buffalo meat is more pronounced in both flavor and taste than beef.

Texture

After ripening and aging, buffalo meat cuts can be made tender. However, they still remain slightly stronger in texture than similar beef cuts.

Fat Content

Buffalo meat is often leaner than beef and the color of buffalo fat is white rather than the yellowish color of fat in beef.

POULTRY MEAT SELECTION AND GRADING

In the global meat market, poultry comes in second after pork. This is due to both its widespread availability and increasing popularity. It also has a competitive production cost. Poultry meat consists of both turkey and chicken.

Turkey meat features darker and brighter muscle components. Processed turkey meat can be used in a variety of products similar to pork and beef, but they are often leaner products. Turkey meat is often processed in two grades.

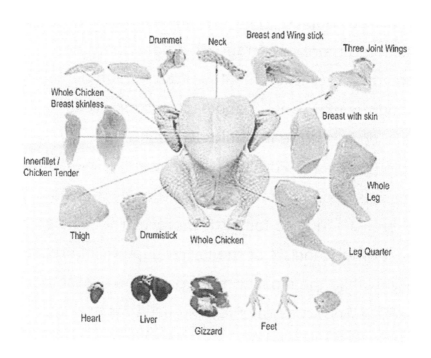

Grade A Turkey

This is top quality turkey meat with no defects on the surface of the meat or the general appearance. These are often used as entire frozen turkey carcasses.

Grade B Turkey

This is often a lower quality of meat that is used for further processing.

In most developing countries, chicken meat is considered more important for production than turkey meat. Chicken meat is often in high demand around popular centers and especially in areas where pork is not eaten for socio-cultural or religious reasons. For chicken meat either the entire carcass is used for fresh meat or the wings, legs and breast are used for further processing. The breast often consists of the larger superficial breast muscle while the smaller more profound breast muscle is known as the filet and used for drying. Chicken meat is graded in four categories.

Grade 1 Chicken - White muscle meat with visible fat, connective tissue and skin removed

This class mostly contains breast and filet meat. It is used for reconstituted chicken hams and sausages.

Grade 2 Chicken - Muscle meat with adhering subcutaneous and intermuscular fat

All chicken cuts that are deboned and skinless fall into this category including breast, legs, and wings. This meat is often chopped or ground to be used for further processing. Often the small amounts of subcutaneous and intermuscular fat aren't removed but incorporated into the final product.

Grade 3 Chicken - Skin and/or fat

Chicken skin is often removed from the carcass or individual cuts and then collected. The skin of a chicken has a high-fat content that can be added to processed meat products. In addition to being added to chicken processed products, it can also be added to meat products to increase flavor and produce a soft texture.

Grade 4 Chicken - Mechanically deboned chicken meat (MDM)

This is a manufactured chicken product that comes by mechanically separating the remaining muscle tissue from a chicken carcass once the legs, wings and breast muscles are removed. MDM can contain chicken necks, muscle meat, connective tissue, and fat. Often MDM won't be used for processed chicken products such as jerky.

Now that we've considered the basics of meat and its processing, it is important to also consider the types of processed meat. While you are only going to be making jerky, it is important to know all categories of processed meats since some regional types of jerky may fall into various categories of processed meats and each needs to be considered differently. So let's briefly consider the definition of various categories of processed meats.

Take a trip to a supermarket or a butcher shop, and you'll likely be overwhelmed by the variety of products, each with their own taste characteristics. In some countries, there may even be hundreds of choices, each with their own characteristics. The only way to better understand these choices and what category your jerky falls into is to consider the definitions of all processed meat. Based on processing techniques and the treatment of the raw material, processed meat fits into six broad groups.

FRESH PROCESSED MEAT PRODUCTS

This category includes any meat mix products that are made up of comminuted muscle meat with a varying amount of animal fat. These products are only salted, but no curing is done. Non-meat ingredients can be added in small quantities for the purpose of flavor and binding improvement. In some low-cost versions, larger quantities of non-meat ingredients can be added to extend volume.

All meat and non-meat ingredients are added to these products in their raw state. Heat treatment in the form of cooking or frying is applied immediately before eating. If the fresh meat is placed in a casing, it is defined as sausages. If the products are portioned, it is known as patties, kebab, etc.

CURED MEAT CUTS

Cured meat comes from entire pieces of muscle meat that are subdivided into one of two groups:

1. Cured-raw meats

2. Cured-cooked meats

The curing process for both is similar. The meat pieces are treated with a small amount of nitrite either in the form of a dry salt or a salt solution in water. The main difference in the two groups is the following:

Cured-raw meats don't undergo a heat treatment during manufacturing. The processing period involves curing, fermentation, and ripening under controlled climate conditions to make the end product palatable. The final product is eaten raw and/or uncooked.

Cured-cooked meats always undergo heat treatment after the curing process to gain desired palatability.

RAW-COOKED MEAT PRODUCTS

These products are made from muscle meat, fat and non-meat ingredients that are processed raw and uncooked by either mixing and/or comminuting. The resulting batter is made into sausages or otherwise heat treated. The heat treatment leads to protein coagulation, which leads to a typical firm-elastic texture.

PRECOOKED-COOKED MEAT PRODUCTS

These products contain a mix of lower-grade muscle trimmings, fatty tissue, head meat, animal feet, skin, blood and other edible slaughter by-products. Two heat treatment procedures are used to manufacture these products. The first treatment is the precooking of raw meat materials and the second is the cooking of the finished product mix at the end of processing.

Precooked-cooked meat products are different from the other categories because the raw materials are precooked before grinding or chopping, but also in the fact that they use a wide variety of meat, by-products and non-meat ingredients.

RAW-FERMENTED SAUSAGES

These are uncooked meat products that contain mixtures of lean meats and fatty tissues along with salts, nitrite, sugars and spices as well as other non-meat ingredients. Everything is filled into casings. The characteristic properties of the ingredients give each sausage a unique flavor, texture, and color through the fermentation process. Shorter or longer ripening phases along with moisture reduction or drying are needed to build up typical flavor and texture for the final product. The final product doesn't undergo heat treatment during processing and is often sold and eaten in raw form.

DRIED MEAT PRODUCTS

These products result from dehydration or drying of lean meat in natural condition or in an artificial environment. Dried meat isn't comparable to fresh meat when it comes to shape, sensory and processing properties; but it results in a longer shelf-life. Most jerky falls into this category.

Let's look more closely at jerky in general and the various types of regional jerky.

JERKY

Meat used to make jerky is often cut into long, thin strips and then dried. Jerky has long been a popular product because it is light, easy to carry, keeps well and provides energy. This is often what makes jerky popular as a snack food and among survivalists.

Jerky can be made from any lean meat, poultry, wild game and even fish. It comes in a variety of flavors with any degree of spice. Jerky can be either smoked or not. The unique flavor you create is up to you, and there are many marinades, brines and spices you can choose from. What is important is choosing lean meats only since fats become rancid in time and can spoil the flavor of the jerky even if it is still safe to eat. This is why venison is one of the best meats for making jerky since it is an extremely lean meat.

JERKY SAFETY

According to USDA guidelines, potentially hazardous food doesn't include a water activity value of 0.85 or less. While jerky is safe at 0.85, molds can still develop on the surface if the air becomes more humid. At 0.70, molds will not grow. Jerky was traditionally just dried and many people still use this same procedure.

In October 2003, the guidelines for making jerky changed after an incidence in 1995 when a small commercial plant in New Mexico experienced an outbreak of Salmonella related to jerky production. 93 people were diagnosed with the disease. The plant drying partially frozen beef strips for three hours at 140 degrees Fahrenheit then holding at 115 degrees Fahrenheit for 19 hours. In the same year, 11 people in Oregon were infected with E.coli from homemade venison jerky. The procedure dried jerky at 125-135 degrees Fahrenheit for 12-18 hours.

As a result of these outbreaks, the Food Safety and Inspection Service instituted a series of policy changes and guidelines. Jerky made from beef should observe the cooking guidelines for beef. What the FSIS concluded is that you need to do more than just following the time-temperature guidelines, but also factor humidity into the cooking process. You need to maintain the relative humidity at 90% or above for at least 25% of the cooking time and no less than an hour. However, homemade jerky production isn't bound by these rules. We'll discuss more about the safety and processing jerky later.

Why Temperature is Important

Heating jerky to 160 degrees Fahrenheit before dehydrating will assure that any bacteria present is destroyed. Most dehydrators don't include this step, and a dehydrator may not reach temperatures high enough to heat the meat to this temperature. It is important to heat meat to 160 degrees Fahrenheit and then maintain a constant dehydrator temperature of 130 to 140 degrees Fahrenheit to achieve two things:

1. The food needs to be dried before it spoils.

2. Enough water needs to be removed so that microorganisms aren't able to grow.

The danger lies in the fact that dehydrating meat and poultry without first cooking it to a safe temperature the dehydrating appliance won't heat the meat to a temperature which kills bacteria before it dries. After drying, bacteria become heat resistant. With a dehydrator or low-temperature oven, most of the heat is absorbed by evaporating moisture. This means the meat doesn't begin to rise in temperature until most of the moisture is evaporated, this means the bacteria are more likely to survive. Pathogenic bacteria can cause foodborne illnesses as a result. The following table shows the recommended drying temperature and time to kill E.coli bacteria.

Temperature	Duration
125 degrees Fahrenheit	10 hours
135 degrees Fahrenheit	8 hours
145 degrees Fahrenheit	7 hours
155 degrees Fahrenheit	4 hours

It is important to note that pork and wild game jerky are at risk of being infected with trichinae and needs to be cooked or treated properly. Again, we'll discuss this in depth later.

The United States Department of Agriculture has defined jerky into four categories:

1. Jerky - This is made from a single piece of meat. It is often labeled as "Natural Style Jerky" and is also labeled with the statement "made from solid pieces of meat."

2. Chunked and Formed Jerky - This is made from chunks that are molded and formed or cut into strips.

3. Ground and Formed or Chopped and Formed Jerky - These two types of jerky are from ground meat that is then molded, pressed or cut into strips.

Let's look at the two main types of whole meat and ground meat jerky.

WHOLE MEAT JERKY

Whole meat or natural beef jerky is what most people associate with the term jerky. It is essentially a dry solid and thin piece of meat that provides a lot of protein and a decent amount of calories. Whole meat jerky has its own character; it is chewable. Initially, the jerky doesn't have much flavor, but as it is chewed the flavor comes out in the jerky. Jerky is an excellent snack for people on the go. Making jerky is simple, but the drying time can be long depending on a variety of factors.

CHOOSING THE MEAT

The most popular beef for making jerky is the flank steak that comes from the abdominal muscles of the cow. In the United States, a flank steak is also known as the London broil.

In general, wild game meat is very lean and makes good jerky. However, there are some safety issues to consider when meat isn't heated to 137 degrees Fahrenheit. The following meats can carry parasites:

➤ Pork from unknown sources.

➤ Wild boar, bear, raccoon and other wild game.

MEAT PREPARATION

For whole meat and natural jerky, you want to use only fresh lean meat. This means you need to remove any visible sinews, silver screen or connective tissues. These parts are good for sausages but make jerky very hard to chew. You should also discard any fat since this can go rancid in time and reduce the flavor of the jerky.

You can cut the meat either with or against the grain. However, some have found that strips cut against the grain make the jerky easier to chew. If you cut across the grain, then the jerky will be more crumbly. Cutting with the grain makes jerky that is easier to chew and takes longer to eat which is what some people prefer. To make the meat easier to cut you should have it partially frozen by placing it in the freezer for two hours.

It doesn't matter how long you cut your jerky strips, but they should only be about 1/4 inch thick. You can cut thicker strips, but these will take longer to dry. Also, these thicker cuts may not fit between dehydrator trays unless you are drying in open air or a smokehouse. For example, South African biltong is a thick sliced jerky.

Before attempting to dry a bigger cut of meat, it is important to research drying meats, microbiology, and safety including adding the right amount of salt and sodium nitrite. You will find that there is a big difference between drying a 1/4 inch jerky strip than a one pound piece of solid meat. For thinner meat, you won't need to add sodium nitrite unless you want a stronger red color or if you plan to smoke the jerky for a long period of time.

MARINATING JERKY

If you marinate meat strips rather than a solid cut of meat, you will get better flavor. There are a number of ready to use marinades that you can choose at the supermarket or you can choose to make your own and experiment with various recipes. When it comes to a good marinade there are three important ingredients:

1. Soy sauce

2. Worcestershire sauce

3. Liquid smoke

Other ingredients you can experiment with in a marinade include the following:

- ❖ Oil

- ❖ Vinegar

- ❖ Tomato ketchup

- ❖ Lemon juice

- ❖ Dry wine

- ❖ Beer

Adding some of these ingredients can also be an added safety factor since they are acidic and will inhibit the growth of bacteria.

You can also add a number of spices to increase the hotness of jerky. Some common ingredients for this include pepper, powdered garlic, and onion. We'll discuss these more in the section on seasonings.

When it comes to marinating beef jerky there are three important things to remember:

1. You should keep marinating meat in the refrigerator.

2. Don't save and re-use marinade.

3. Marinated jerky strips will dry faster.

Marinated natural jerky is best if it is stored in a sealed container for one to two weeks at room temperature. If kept in the refrigerator it can be good up to six months. Or if you freeze it, it will last up to twelve months. You can choose to vacuum seal your jerky for consumers to help extend the shelf life.

One popular way of marinating jerky is to brine it. There isn't a universal brine recipe, and you'll often get customized instructions from a variety of sources. This is because different salts have different densities and weights such as table salt and kosher salt. You can have complete control if you choose to make your own brine. There are two things you need in order to make your own brine.

Brine Tester

These products consist of a float with a stem attached and markings in degrees. The instrument floats at its highest level when placed in a saturated brine while reading 100 degrees or a 26.4% salt solution. In a weaker brine, the stem will float at lower levels with a lower reading. If no salt is present the reading will be 0. This will help you to see how much salt you are adding to your water and what level your brine is at. However, it is important to keep in mind that when you add other ingredients, this instrument will only measure the density of the solution and not the actual salinity of the brine you are making.

Brine Tables

It is important that you learn how to use a brine table if you are going to make your own jerky brine. There are many advantages to using these tables including the following:

➢ You can calculate the strength of any recipe.

➢ You can determine how much salt to add to a gallon of water in order to make a specific strength.

> You don't have to worry about the type of salt you are using when making your brine.

Consider the following brine table and how it came make your process simpler:

Brine Table for Brine at 60 Degrees Fahrenheit in US Gallons

Salometer Degrees	% Salt by Weight	Lbs. of Salt per Gallon of H2O	Lbs. of Salt per Gallon of Brine	Lbs. of Water per Gallon of Brine
0	0.000	0.000	0.000	8.328
1	0.264	0.022	0.022	8.323
2	0.526	0.044	0.044	8.317
3	0.792	0.066	0.066	8.307
4	1.056	0.089	0.089	8.298

5	1.320	0.111	0.111	8.292
6	1.584	0.134	0.133	8.286
7	1.848	0.157	0.156	8.280
8	2.112	0.180	0.178	8.274
9	2.376	0.203	0.201	8.268
10	2.640	0.226	0.224	8.262
11	2.903	0.249	0.247	8.256
12	3.167	0.272	0.270	8.250
13	3.431	0.296	0.293	8.239
14	3.695	0.320	0.316	8.229
15	3.959	0.343	0.339	8.222

16	4.223	0.367	0.362	8.216
17	4.487	0.391	0.386	8.209
18	4.751	0.415	0.409	8.202
19	5.015	0.440	0.433	8.195
20	5.279	0.464	0.456	8.188
21	5.543	0.489	0.480	8.181
22	5.807	0.513	0.504	8.174
23	6.071	0.538	0.528	8.167
24	6.335	0.563	0.552	8.159
25	6.599	0.588	0.576	8.152
26	6.863	0.614	0.600	8.144

27	7.127	0.639	0.624	8.137
28	7.391	0.665	0.649	8.129
29	7.655	0.690	0.673	8.121
30	7.919	0.716	0.698	8.113
31	8.162	0.742	0.722	8.105
32	8.446	0.768	0.747	8.097
33	8.710	0.795	0.772	8.089
34	8.974	0.821	0.797	8.081
35	9.238	0.848	0.822	8.073
36	9.502	0.874	0.847	8.064
37	9.766	0.901	0.872	8.056

38	10.030	0.928	0.897	8.047
39	10.294	0.956	0.922	8.038
40	10.558	0.983	0.948	8.030
41	10.822	1.011	0.973	8.021
42	11.086	1.038	0.999	8.012
43	11.350	1.066	1.025	8.003
44	11.614	1.094	1.050	7.994

45	11.878	1.123	1.076	7.985
46	12.142	1.151	1.102	7.975
47	12.406	1.179	1.128	7.966
48	12.670	1.208	1.154	7.957
49	12.934	1.237	1.181	7.947
50	13.198	1.266	1.207	7.937
51	13.461	1.295	1.233	7.928

52	13.725	1.325	1.260	7.918
53	13.989	1.355	1.286	7.908
54	14.253	1.384	1.313	7.898
55	14.517	1.414	1.340	7.888
56	14.781	1.444	1.368	7.878
57	15.045	1.475	1.393	7.867
58	15.309	1.505	1.420	7.857

59	15.573	1.536	1.447	7.847
60	15.837	1.567	1.475	7.836
61	16.101	1.598	1.502	7.826
62	16.365	1.630	1.529	7.815
63	16.629	1.661	1.557	7.804
64	16.893	1.693	1.584	7.793
65	17.157	1.725	1.612	7.782

66	17.421	1.757	1.639	7.771
67	17.685	1.789	1.668	7.764
68	17.949	1.822	1.697	7.756
69	18.213	1.854	1.725	7.744
70	18.477	1.887	1.753	7.733
71	18.740	1.921	1.781	7.721
72	19.004	1.954	1.809	7.710

73	19.268	1.988	1.837	7.698
74	19.532	2.021	1.866	7.686
75	19.796	2.056	1.895	7.678
76	20.060	2.090	1.925	7.669
77	20.324	2.124	1.953	7.657
78	20.588	2.159	1.982	7.645
79	20.852	2.194	2.011	7.633

80	21.116	2.229	2.040	7.621
81	21.380	2.265	2.069	7.608
82	21.644	2.300	2.098	7.596
83	21.908	2.336	2.128	7.586
84	22.172	2.372	2.159	7.577
85	22.436	2.409	2.188	7.584
86	22.700	2.446	2.217	7.551

87	22.964	2.482	2.248	7.542
88	23.228	2.520	2.279	7.532
89	23.492	2.557	2.309	7.519
90	23.756	2.595	2.338	7.505
91	24.019	2.633	2.368	7.492
92	24.283	2.671	2.398	7.479
93	24.547	2.709	2.430	7.468

94	24.811	2.748	2.461	7.458
95	25.075	2.787	2.491	7.444
96	25.339	2.826	2.522	7.430
97	25.603	2.866	2.552	7.416
98	25.867	2.908	2.570	7.409
99	26.131	2.948	2.616	7.394
99.6	26.289	2.970	2.634	7.385

100	26.395	2.986	2.647	7.380

Making Brine

When it comes to making brine here are a few questions you need to ask first:

1. Depending on the weight of your meat, how much brine do you need?

2. Depending on the kind of meat and curing time, how strong of a brine do you need?

3. Do you need a nitrate or a nitrite?

4. Do you need sugar?

Let's carefully consider each of these and impact they have on you making a brine for your jerky.

How Much Brine

The simplest way is to estimate the amount of brine you need. You need enough to cover the meats, and you'll waste a lot of brine if you cure a small amount of meat in a large container. The basic rule is to use about 50% brine related to the weight of the meat. For example, if you have two pounds of meat you should have one pound of brine.

It is also best to use a container that has a size and shape that will accommodate the meat while also having you use as little brine as possible. From here you can choose the strength of the brine and adding salt while reading the salometer. However, you can save time by simply using the table.

In order to make the brine, you only need to use three of the columns from the table. For example, if you want 22 degrees of brine for a chicken then you follow the 22-degree row. In column three you will see that you need to add 0.513 lb of salt to a gallon of water. Check it with your salinometer and you can add a cup of water or a tablespoon of salt in order to get the ideal reading.

Other times you'll need to make a specific amount of brine to fit a specific container. To make a specific amount of brine you'll want to use columns four and five. For example, if you have a ten-gallon container and you want to fill it with 60-degree brine then column 5 shows that you need 1.475 pounds of salt to make one gallon of brine and column 7 shows that 0.941 gallons of water is needed. You then need to multiple the readings by 10 gallons.

Brine Strength

You won't find a universal brine or strength, it is entirely up to you. This is why it is important to have a brine tester and a notebook for you to record results for future reference. If you are going to have a shorter curing time, you'll want a stronger brine, or you can increase your curing time and use a milder brine. Consider the table below to give you a general idea of a good brine strength based on the meat you are using:

Brine Strength	Meat Product
20	Chicken
30	Poultry & Fish
40	Chicken
50	Spareribs

60	Bacon & Loins
60-80	Hams & Shoulders
80	Fish

It is important to note that if you add sugar, a brine will become heavier. For example, if you add eight pounds of salt to five gallons of water you get a 61-degree brine. However, if you add three pounds of sugar to the mix, then you get 75 degrees brine.

The method of curing you use, the time you cure the meat and the brine strength all have an impact on each other. Keep the following three tips in mind:

1. The stronger your brine, the faster the curing action.

2. The larger the meat, the more brining time is required.

3. Pumping meat will shorten the curing time versus simply brining.

You should make sure you don't brine meats that have already been brined before you purchase them. When it comes to estimating curing times consider the following general guidelines:

➢ 11 days per inch of thickness

➢ About 3 1/2 to 4 days per pound for twenty pounds

➢ 3 days per pound for smaller cuts

The following table is to help orient you to curing times based on brine strength, but you can improvise based on your brine.

Meat	Brine Strength	Time
Meat (Ham & Shoulders)	65-75 Degrees	4 Days per Pound

Bacon	55-65 Degrees	1 1/2 - 2 Days per Pound
Loins	55-65 Degrees	3 Weeks
Spareribs	50-55 Degrees	1 Week
Poultry	21 Degrees	Overnight
Fish	80 Degrees	1/2 - 2 Hours

Nitrates or Nitrites

When it comes to a wet cure, the USDA regulations allow for the following amounts of nitrates/nitrites:

➢ Seven pounds of sodium or potassium nitrate to 100-gallon pickle

➢ Two pounds of sodium or potassium nitrite to 100-gallon pickle at 10% pump le

The first thing you need to answer is whether you are going to use nitrate or nitrite. If you are going to cook or smoke your meats at 190 degrees Fahrenheit or higher, then you won't need to worry about botulism. Nitrates/nitrites will prevent botulism, but also impart a specific flavor and color to smoked meats.

The amount of nitrate will always stay the same no matter what brine strength you use as long as there is one gallon of water and it conforms to the government established 200 ppm maximum limit. The brine table can help you make sure recipes conform to government standards.

Since meat may be soaked in brine for a while, you want to make sure the brine is very clean otherwise you can introduce bacteria and spoil the brine. This is why you should consider pre-curing your meat. You can do this by taking part of a dry curing mix and rubbing it into the meat. Allow it to sit overnight in a cool place such as the refrigerator to draw out the blood. Then rinse the meat and immerse it in the brine.

Next, dissolve the required amount of salt in water and bring to a boil. Allow it to boil for about an hour since prolonged boiling will kill bacteria. Transfer some of the brine to a smaller container along with any non-meat ingredients. Add this small amount to the main brine portion and check it with a brine tester for appropriate strength. Allow it to sit for 24-48 hours so impurities can settle to the bottom. Siphon the solution through a filter such as fine cloth, paper towel or gauze into another container without stirring up the sediment on the bottom. Ideally, the brine shouldn't be stored at any temperatures above four degrees Celsius.

This procedure may sound like a lot of work, but it is important to do this with large amounts of brine. If you are going to be curing large amounts of meat you don't want to risk contaminating the brine. For smaller amounts of meat, you likely won't need to go through this process, but should still check with a brine tester and keep the mixture refrigerated until use.

Sugar

Sugar isn't a curing agent, and the main use in jerky is to offset the harshness of the salt while improving flavor and the final color. Sugar in a low concentration while meat curing will help prevent the growth of bacteria. When sugar is added to brine, it becomes food for bacteria. If no sugar is present, the bacteria will often feed on the meat protein.

Sugar also has the benefit of helping to develop color. It does this indirectly by providing food to the bacteria that react with nitrate to release nitrite. In addition, sugar acts as an antioxidant. This allows the sugar to react with oxygen that would otherwise change the color of the meat.

When you add sugar to a curing solution, it should stay at a temperature below 41 degrees Fahrenheit. Anything above this temperature will cause rapid fermentation and lead to the development of microorganisms that could spoil the meat. Even at low temperatures, adding sugar to a wet cure needs to be limited to 2% in relation to the salt to avoid rapid fermentation that can affect the final quality of the jerky product.

Typically the accepted use is about 1-2% of sugar in a wet cure solution and 2-2.5% of sugar in a dry cure mix. It doesn't matter whether you use brown or white sugar. Typically, meat curing uses beet, cane and corn sugars. Sometimes molasses and syrups are also used. It is important to note that different sugars have different levels of sweetness. Honey is often used with lean meats or even bacon because of the distinctive flavor it offers.

Bad Brine

The bad brine will show with one of four symptoms:

1. White slime and foam on top.

2. Milky color and foul odor.

3. Blue in color.

4. Tacky to touch.

It is normal for a thin scum or white mold to accumulate on the brine. You should periodically remove this foam. If the foam starts to give off a foul odor, turn blue or become thicker, then you'll have to remove the meat and wash it in cool water before placing it in new brine.

Anytime you suspect a brine has spoiled you should replace it with a fresh solution right away. Most of the time there is nothing wrong with the meat, you'll just need to rinse it first. Cured meats needed to be completely immersed in brine and weighed down if needed. No meat should stick out of the brine since it can spoil and ruin the entire solution.

If you are going to be brining large amounts of meat you should place heavy pieces of meat at the bottom and lighter ones on top. Meat should also be packed skin side down with a suitable clean weight on top to prevent the meat from contacting the air.

The containers should be placed in the refrigerator or at least in a cool, well-ventilated location.

Reusing Brine

It is generally not a good idea to reuse brine since some bacteria can exist from the previous use. In addition, most cure mixes are so cheap that you shouldn't risk the meat contamination. Even if brine is going to be reused, it needs to have professional testing, and this is often only recommended for commercial meat plants and large production plants.

Another popular option for jerky making is ground meat jerky. Let's consider this next.

GROUND MEAT JERKY

Another option for making jerky is to make it from ground meat. Most choose to buy 93% lean meat and then grind it through a 1/4 inch grinder plate. If you choose this option, you should only use lean meat and remove any visible sinews, silver screen, and connective tissue. In jerky, these parts will make it hard to chew. You should also discard any fat since it can go rancid in time and reduce the flavor of the jerky. It is important that you use as fresh meat as possible since ground meat contains more bacteria than whole meat strips.

The process of making ground meat jerky is very similar to the process for fresh sausages. The raw meat is ground, then mixed with spices, stuffed in a tube and squeezed out of a jerky gun into strips. Let's look at each of these steps.

First, you want to grind the meat and mix it with spices. You should add 1.8% salt in relation to the meat weight. This comes out to 18 g salt per 1 kg of meat. After adding the salt, mix it well by kneading the mixture hard until it becomes sticky. You can add Worcestershire sauce or other liquid ingredients that go well with all types of jerky. You can also choose to add tomato ketchup, vinegar or lemon juice; all of these are acidic and can help inhibit the growth of bacteria.

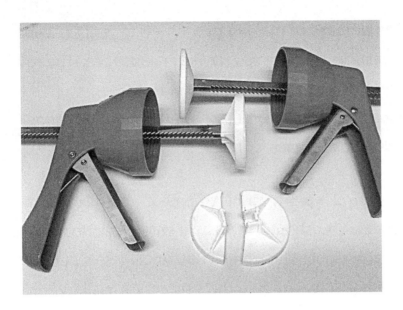

These ingredients can be mixed in a variety of proportions, and it's largely up to you. However, keep in mind that the more moisture you add, the longer the drying time; but it will add new flavors that enhance your jerky while also making it easier to force out of the jerky gun. We'll discuss more about additives in non-meat ingredients later.

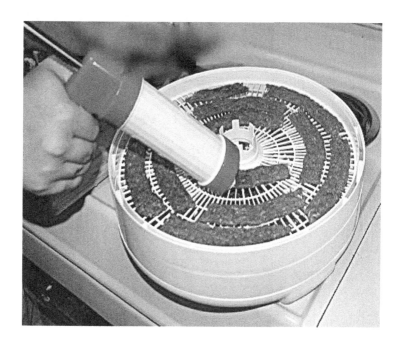

The jerky is then formed by a specially designed jerky gun that you can buy from many on and offline retailers. Once you've made the jerky strips you want to place them on a screen and dry them in a dehydrator. The drying time will depend on the meat thickness, temperature, humidity and your type of dehydrator. After the jerky is dried completely, remove any spots of oil with a paper towel. Allow the jerky to cool and then package appropriately.

Storing dried jerky in a sealed container it will be good for one to two weeks at room temperature, six months in a refrigerator and twelve months in a freezer. You can also choose to vacuum package the jerky in order to increase shelf life.

WILD GAME JERKY

When you make jerky from the wild game, you should pre-cook it to 165 degrees Fahrenheit. Most game meats are often infected with trichinae and other parasites. If you don't cook the meat, then you want to freeze it according to USDA rules. Freezing meat will help with trichinae, but won't get rid of bacteria. To increase the safety of your wild game jerky you want to make sure you do the following:

✓ Good manufacturing practices

✓ At least 2% salt

✓ Sodium nitrite

✓ Dry cure the jerky

✓ Use acidic ingredients in your brine marinade

✓ Don't make jerky strips thicker than 1/4 inch

In addition to whole meat and ground meat jerky, there are two traditional methods of jerky making that are still used today and are popular in some regions. Let's take a look at biltong and pemmican jerky.

BILTONG

Biltong is a type of jerky popular in South Africa that is made by drying meat. The name biltong comes from the Dutch word Bil meaning buttock and Tong meaning strip. Biltong is made by salting, spicing and curing selected meat cuts. It is often made using beef, venison, kudu, springbok or ostrich. Consider the following table to see how biltong and traditional jerky are the same, yet different.

Procedure	Jerky	Biltong
Heat Treatment	Yes	No
Vinegar	Optional	Yes
Smoked	Optional	No

Air Dried	Yes	Yes

When it comes to biltong, the cuts are often bigger and thicker than jerky. The thicker the meat you are working with, the longer it will take to dry; thus increasing the risk of spoilage.

Homemade biltong typically uses beef buttock. The best cuts are sirloin and steaks from the hip, typically known as the topside or silverside. The best biltong comes from the eye of the round muscles down both sides of the backbone. Ideally, the meat should be marinated in a vinegar solution for a few hours and then poured off before flavoring the meat. The dominant spice used in biltong is coriander.

Drying meat such as biltong is easier than drying salami. Jerky is the easiest to dry as the strips are smaller and can be dried fast. You don't have to worry about controlling the humidity. Biltong flavor

is determined by the meat quality and the
marinade.

PEMMICAN

Pemmican is a form of jerky that was used by the Native Indians. Pemmican is a form of high energy bar that lasts for years. Traditional pemmican doesn't contain pork but is often made from large animals such a buffalo, venison, moose and elk. There are four distinct aspects to pemmican that make it unique.

1. The sliced meat is either dried over a fire or in the sun.

2. The dried meat is pounded with a wooden mallet or ground and shredded between stones.

3. The pulverized meat is often combined with ground berries, peppermint leaves and/or onions for added flavor.

4. The mixture often contains melted fat and bone marrow grease.

The hot mixture was traditionally poured into a large buffalo-hide bag and allowed to cool and harden. Holes were burned in the hide for strings to allow the bag to be opened and closed. The bags were prepared in a way to keep out air and moisture. The pemmican could be kept fresh for years. The pemmican was chopped off with an ax and eaten raw or boiled.

One thing that pemmican shows is that you can add a number of non-meat ingredients to jerky. So let's move on to considering the various non-meat ingredients you can choose to add to your jerky to make it unique

NON-MEAT INGREDIENTS IN JERKY

Along with the two main components of beef jerky (meat and fat), a wide range of non-meat ingredients can be used. Some of these ingredients are necessary such as salt and spices. Other ingredients are used to make specific jerky products such as biltong and pemmican. The best way to categorize non-meat jerky ingredients is by the source, creating three categories:

1. Chemical substances

2. Plant ingredients

3. Animal based ingredients

Another way to classify these ingredients is whether they are additives or full foods. Still another option is to categorize them as having functional properties or not.

ADDITIVES

These are often substances that aren't eaten as food but can be added for a specific technological and quality characteristic. This would be things such as salt, curing agents, spices, water binding and gelatin enhancing substances.

Most ingredients are functional, meaning they have the ability to introduce or improve certain characteristics of the jerky. These ingredients will have an impact on one or more of the following:

✓ Taste

✓ Flavor

✓ Appearance

✓ Color

✓ Texture

✓ Water Binding

✓ Counteracting Fat Separation

✓ Preservation

Ingredients that are purely functional without any other effects such as filling or extending the volume of the final product are typically only used in small amounts. The criteria that functional non-meat ingredients need to meet are two things:

1. Safe for consumers

2. Improve processing technology and/or sensory quality of the finished product

In addition to functional substances, there is another group of ingredients that aren't intended to change the appearance of the final product or make quality improvements. Rather these ingredients serve to add volume to meat products. These are known as meat extenders and fillers. They serve the purpose of making meat products cheaper. The ingredients typically include the following:

✓ Cereals

✓ Legumes

- ✓ Vegetables

- ✓ Roots

- ✓ Tubers

These ingredients are typically used in larger quantities, averaging between two and fifteen percent.

MEAT EXTENDERS

These typically come from plant proteins; often legumes such as soybeans being the main source. These cheap plant proteins are used to extend the more expensive meat proteins while still preserving the overall protein contents of meat products. However, these extenders may also affect the quality of the final product. Other extenders can come from animal protein sources such as whole milk and eggs.

FILLERS

Fillers are made mostly from plant substances. They are often high in carbohydrates and low in protein. Most often they are cereals, roots, tubers, and vegetables. Occasionally they will come from refined products like starches and flours. If you get a pure meat product, it will be very low in carbohydrates. In addition to the volume filling capacity of these products, some fillers such as starches and flours; are also used for their ability to absorb large amounts of water.

Extenders and Fillers aren't a standard ingredient in processed meats, and most high-quality jerky products are often made without them. However, they can be a helpful tool when it comes to cost reduction.

BINDERS

Another definition of non-meat ingredients is binders. This can apply to ingredients of both animal and plant origin that have a high level of protein and serve the purpose of either water and/or fat binding. These substances often have a high-protein soy, wheat and/or milk product such as soy isolate, wheat gluten or milk protein.

These aren't the same as extenders because they are in too low quantities, but their high-quality proteins do help with water binding and protein network structuring. Although some of the substances such as starches and flours listed above under fillers can bind water and fat by physical entrapment.

As you can see from these three definitions, there are a wide range of non-meat ingredients. It can be quite difficult to define these ingredients. Most substances have a single dominating effect, but most have desirable side effects that can make them difficult to define. For example, texture vegetable protein is primarily used for the non-functional purpose of meat extension, but it also has a water binding effect that makes it moderately functional.

This is why it can sometimes be easier to list non-meat ingredients by their origin and divide them into the categories of chemical, animal or plant origin.

CHEMICAL INGREDIENTS

There are a number of chemical ingredients that have been approved for use in food processing. Although when it comes to meat processing, most countries limit the number of approved chemicals. The following are the most significant chemical ingredients:

✓ Salt - Taste, impact on meat protein and shelf-life.

✓ Nitrite - Curing color, flavor, and shelf-life.

✓ Ascorbic Acid - Accelerate curing reaction.

✓ Phosphates - Protein structuring and water binding.

✓ Chemical Preservatives - Shelf-life.

✓ Antioxidants - Flavor and shelf-life.

✓ Monosodium Glutamate (MSG) - Flavor enhancement.

✓ Food Coloring - Synthetic and of plant origin.

Most chemical ingredients serve functional purposes and are used in small amounts, often under 1%. Only salt is sometimes used in the range of 2-4%.

ANIMAL ORIGIN INGREDIENTS

Animal origin ingredients aren't that common, but can sometimes be used in specific meat preparations. All of these ingredients have functional properties with the exception of whole milk. In particular, these ingredients help with water binding and prevent fat separation during heat treatment. In addition to their functional properties, some animal ingredients can also be used as meat extenders. Some common animal origin ingredients include the following:

✓ Milk Caseinate - 90% protein, used in 2% or less quantities; used for fat and water binding properties.

✓ Whole Milk or Non-fat Dried Milk - Used in some regional meat preparations as a protein extender.

✓ Gelatin - Used for binding properties and as a meat extender.

✓ Blood Plasma - Used for binding purposes.

✓ Eggs - Often used in sausages as an extender and binding ingredient.

✓ Transglutaminase - Used for binding purposes.

PLANT ORIGIN INGREDIENTS

All jerky spices fall into the plant origin category. These ingredients are primarily functional and used in small quantities for the purpose of adding flavor and taste to jerky. However, there are some plant origin ingredients that are high in protein and used as binders in order to increase water binding and fat retention for intensely heat treated meat products. Two of the most commonly used binders are isolated soy protein at 90% protein and wheat gluten at 80% protein. Some lesser used plant ingredients for binding include protein isolates that come from legumes.

Other plant origin ingredients can be used as meat extenders or fillers. Meat extenders are often high in protein while fillers are high in carbohydrates. This is more common in sausages and other meat preparations rather than jerky since they are used to replace expensive meat in lower to medium grade meat products in order to increase volume.

The three most common meat extenders are the following:

1. Soy flour at 50% protein.

2. Soy concentrate at 70% protein.

3. Food legumes such as beans, peas, lentils in specific meat products.

Fillers or carbohydrate products with a low protein content are usually used in 2-15% quantities such as roots and vegetables. Typical fillers include the following:

- ✓ Cereal flours - wheat, rice, and corn.

- ✓ Starches - wheat, rice, corn, potato, and cassava.

- ✓ Breadcrumbs

- ✓ Rusk - a result of mixing and baking wheat flour.

- ✓ Cereals - added without milling.

- ✓ Roots and tubers - cassava, sweet potato.

- ✓ Vegetables and fruits - commonly onion, bell pepper, carrots, green vegetables and bananas.

- ✓ Polysaccharides

- ✓ Carrageenan

USING NON-MEAT INGREDIENTS

There are a number of methods that can be used to add the above ingredients to meat products. The methods used will depend on the properties of the ingredient and the intended meat product. To get the equal flavor, color, texture and/or any other characteristic of the end product you will need to choose a method that provides uniform distribution.

APPLICATION METHODS

During Grinding

Chemical ingredients and small quantities of fine or coarse non-meat ingredients or substances are best added into ground meat products by mixing them with the raw materials before grinding. For homemade ground jerky products, this is simply mixed and then passed through the grinder plates.

During Chopping

If you are going to be making finely comminuted or chopped jerky, then you can easily disperse non-meat ingredients by mixing them with the rest of the batter in the comminuting equipment. This is common when adding binders.

Application to Non-Comminuted Meat

If you need to add non-meat ingredients to large meat pieces or intact muscles such as whole meat jerky or biltong, then you have a more complex operation. You can choose to inject the ingredients as a part of the curing brine, but this will only work if the ingredients are water soluble or can be easily dispersed in water. This option is the most rapid method for equal distribution.

Another option is a surface application if the ingredients are dry substances. For dry substances you can also immerse the meat in salt/curing salt and flavoring solutions. However, for immersion, the process will take days or weeks to get the ingredients diffused throughout the muscle tissue.

PROPERTIES OF NON-MEAT INGREDIENTS

When you start to make your own jerky products, it is important that you know the key characteristics and properties of non-meat ingredients. This will help guide you to choosing the right non-meat ingredients and keeping your jerky all natural. So let's look at some of the most common substances frequently used in jerky making.

Salt (Sodium Chloride)

This ingredient is typically used at levels of 1.5-3%. Salt is one of the most common ingredients used in meat production since it contributes to the final taste of the product. Salt when combined with water also helps with opening up the protein structures. Proteins gel upon heating, and when the moisture and fats are entrapped, they provide form, structure, and firmness to the final product. Lastly, salt is used to improve the water holding capacity of meat.

Seasonings and Spices

When you make your own jerky, you'll find that seasonings and spices are indispensable. Your choice of seasoning and spices is what makes your jerky unique and all through the addition of natural plant products so you can maintain a completely natural jerky product. Let's look at some of the seasoning options.

Seasonings are typically plant-based ingredients that help enhance the flavor of jerky and provide it with a unique flavor. This is where your creativity will have to shine; you need to put your Chef hat on and come up with a few unique flavors and taste that will make you stand out among the all jerky making businesses.

Natural Spices

This category of spices includes dried rootstocks, barks, flowers, fruits and/or seeds. Some of the most common natural spices used in jerky making include the following:

✓ Pepper

✓ Paprika

✓ Nutmeg

✓ Mace

✓ Cloves

✓ Ginger

✓ Cinnamon

✓ Cardamom

✓ Chili

✓ Coriander

✓ Cumin

✓ Pimento

Herbs

Herbs are often the dried leaves of plants. The most common herbs used in jerky making include the following:

✓ Basil

✓ Celery

✓ Marjoram

✓ Oregano

✓ Rosemary

✓ Thyme

Vegetable Bulbs

The two main vegetable bulbs used in natural jerky making include onions and garlic.

Extracts

When it comes to natural spices, you'll often hear about extracts. This is because most natural spices contain high numbers of microorganisms, particularly spores, due to their production process. For meat products, this can create problems with stability. You can reduce this microbial load through irradiation or fumigation. These treatments aren't allowed everywhere, and for those who want a natural jerky, it is better to use extracts.

Extracts are derived by separating the flavor intense portions of a plant through physicochemical procedures such as steam distillation. This gives you a germ-free flavoring substance. Extracts are often preferred and come in liquid or oil forms.

Processing and Handling Spices

Most spices used in jerky making are typically ground or milled. The milling method can affect the quality of the spices. More typically, spices are cold-milled at low temperatures. Raw spices are deep-frozen, preventing the loss of oleoresins, aqua-resins and essential oils which are the valuable flavor components. When working with spices, you need to do the following:

❖ All spices should be kept in a cool, dark and dry place.

❖ Spices should be kept in tightly sealed containers or bags to avoid flavor loss.

❖ You should only remove spices from storage with a spice spoon. Avoid using your hands since this will result in moisture and germs contaminating the spices; causing a loss of flavor or clotting of dry mixes.

❖ When working with spices, you should add them by exact weight in order to have a standard flavor and taste for the finished product.

❖ If a product is going to be eaten hot, then the spices should be prepared mildly.

❖ If you are adding spices to a product under high temperature, then you want strong seasonings.

Let's consider the following table to show you want common seasonings are used and how they work.

Spice	Use
Black/White Pepper	Used in nearly all meat products
Paprika	Used in frankfurters, minced meats, and other products. Sometimes used as a coloring agent
Chili	Used for spice purposes
Pimento	Has an aroma similar to nutmeg, cinnamon, and cloves. Used often in sausages. Can be used as a replacement for black pepper in smoked jerky products.
Mace	Typically used in sausages, frankfurters, and bologna

	or similar products.
Ginger	Used in frankfurters or similar products.
Nutmeg	Used in Bologna, minced sausages, frankfurters and gelatinous meat products.
Clove	Used in Bologna, gelatinous meat mixes, and sausages.
Cinnamon	Astringent and sweet, used in some regions as a seasoning for a variety of meat products, including jerky.
Cardamom	During storage, it can rapidly lose aromatic constituents. Used often in sausages and gelatinous

	meat mixes.
Celery Seed	Typically only used in fresh pork sausages.
Coriander Seed	Contains 13% fatty matter and some tannin. Often found in lunch meats and sausages. Popular in biltong.
Cumin	Offers a distinct flavor to all meat products.
Marjoram and Thyme	Often used in liver and raw-cooked sausages along with gelatinous meat mixes
Onion	Used in a variety of meat products. Sometimes used as a garlic replacement.

Garlic	Used in many types of meat products.

Water

Water is a main component in meat, in fact, learn meat is 80% water. This means that all meat products contain either a lower or higher amount of natural water. Water is also added to many processed meat products. However, this doesn't mean that water is simply added to increase weight. Water is actually added for technical reasons or to compensate for loss during cooking.

When it comes to raw-cooked meat batters, water acts with salt and phosphates to solubilize muscle proteins. This creates a strong protein network structure that keeps the product together after heat treatment.

For Precooked-cooked meat mixes, water is used to compensate for cooking loss; which can be up to

30%. This prevents that final product from being too dry. However, too much water added can cause fat and jelly separation in the end product.

As a jerky maker, water is often used as a substrate for curing substances or other non-meat ingredients. It can also be used for re-hydration of meat extenders.

Nitrite/Nitrates

Small quantities of 0.01-0.03% nitrite/nitrate ingredients will help produce the desired color in processed meat products. Without nitrite/nitrate, meat can turn a gray color when heated. For canned meat products, nitrite can help inhibit microbial growth. However, when it comes to natural jerky, this ingredient has been the source of some controversy. Let's take a closer look at this ingredient.

In the past is was discovered that salt with a higher nitrate content gave the meat a different color and taste. In addition, rock salts mined within different parts of the world had different properties based on the impurities within. Today, the Food and Drug Administration has established limits on the use of nitrates and nitrites because they are considered powerful poisons. So why are they still used to make jerky?

This is because, through modern science testing and experiments, there is no better way to cure meats and prevent food poisoning. There are four main reasons nitrates and nitrites are still used in meat making:

1. They preserve meat's natural color.

2. They impart a characteristic flavor to cured meats.

3. They prevent the transformation of botulinum spores into toxins and eliminate the risk of food poisoning.

4. They prevent rancidity of fats.

Nitrate or Nitrite?

The USDA allows both nitrates and nitrites in the curing of meat and poultry, with the exception of bacon where nitrate use is prohibited. Throughout the world, sodium nitrate is a commonly used meat cure. In fact, most cures contain both nitrite and nitrate.

The fact is there is nearly no difference between the two. No matter which you use, the results are nearly the same. The biggest difference is the fact that pure sodium nitrite is a stronger poison than nitrate. Nitrite is more desired since it is predictable and easier to control dosing when curing meats. Nitrite is also effective at low temperatures. When meats are cured at low temperatures the growth of bacteria is slowed and the shelf life of the product is extended.

If nitrates are used then salt penetration is often ahead of color development. This results in large pieces of meat being too salty once they are fully colored and they will need to be soaked in water. This problem is eliminated when using nitrite.

Nitrite is faster, and the color mixes before the salt fully penetrates the meat.

The Law of Nitrate Use

The law limits the ingoing nitrite and nitrate limits in PPM or parts per million. The following table shows the limits set by the US Food Safety and Inspection Service.

Agent	Immersion Cure	Massaged or Pumped	Comminuted	Dry Cured
Sodium Nitrite	200	200	156	625
Potassi	200	200	156	625

um Nitrite				
Sodium Nitrate	700	700	1718	2187
Potassium Nitrate	700	700	1718	2187

Safety Concerns

The general public has recently seen much concern over the consumption of nitrates. Studies were published that showed nitrites when combined with by-products of protein lead to the formation of nitrosamines, which are known carcinogens in laboratory animals. Studies also found a link between nitrates to cure bacon and the development of nitrosamines when cooked.

However, in order to reach the required temperatures for this to happen, you would need to cook your meat to a temperature of 600 degrees Fahrenheit. Most jerky products are smoked or cooked to a temperature no higher than 200 degrees Fahrenheit, so they aren't affected by these studies. There have been no studies that prove nitrates and nitrites when used within established limits pose a danger to human health.

Ascorbic Acid, Sodium Ascorbate, Erythorbate

Ascorbic acid is better known as Vitamin C. Sodium ascorbate is the more stable salt form or the chemical equivalent of a cheap sodium erythorbate. These ingredients are often used as cure accelerators and are typically added to curing salt. These substances work to accelerate the reaction of nitrite with the red muscle pigments, resulting in the red curing color. Meat products such as jerky that are heat treated during manufacture, instantly develop a red curing color and is intensified by cure accelerators.

Phosphates

Phosphates are often used at levels of 0.05-0.5%. They have a wide application in meat processing to help with binding and texture. They work to directly increase the water holding capacity through the raising of pH. Phosphates also help to stabilize the texture of meat through an increase in protein solubility in connection with salt. In addition, it works to reduce lipid oxidation/rancidity which can result in negative flavors. Phosphates have also been shown to reduce microbial growth.

Sugars

Sugars are often added to jerky to provide a specific flavor and counteract the salty flavor. Larger amounts of sugar can be found in Asian style meat products where they lower water activity and extend the shelf-life. In Western style products, sugar is typically used as a taste and flavor enhancement.

FLAVOR ENHANCERS

If you are going to make natural jerky, you'll likely want to stick with natural seasonings rather than flavor enhancers, but we'll talk about them for a brief moment. These ingredients are intended to intensify the flavor characteristics of meat products. An example of this would be MSG which is popular in Asia.

FOOD COLORING

Using food coloring to change the color of fresh or processed meats isn't a very common practice. It is often only done to get the characteristic red color of processed meats during the curing process. The process of curing isn't about dying the meat, but the chemical reaction of the red muscle pigment with nitrite does result in a stable red color that doesn't change while storing or heating the meat.

PRESERVATIVES

When it comes to processing meats, the preferred method of preservation includes the appropriate application of good slaughter, meat handling, and processing hygiene. When complying with these requirements, bacterial counts are kept low and chemical preservatives shouldn't be needed.

Chemical preservatives can be a sensitive issue, especially if you want to make natural jerky. However, they can be an important and valuable ingredient in meat handling and processing in order to extend the shelf life of meat to reduce losses.

Often the conventional additives for the purpose of reddening, binding or flavoring meat also have moderate antimicrobial effects. Nitrate and Phosphate are two of the most common ingredients. Common salt also has antimicrobial effects.

However, this is enough of the particulars of meat and processing. Let's get into what you came here for and look at the actual process of making natural jerky.

THE JERKY MAKING PROCESS

Making jerky is a relatively simple process. Currently, the USDA recommends heating the meat to 160 degrees Fahrenheit before beginning the dehydration process. Doing this will make sure that present bacteria is destroyed by either wet or moist heat. Most dehydrators don't include this step and often doesn't reach temperatures high enough to heat meat properly. So you want to cook the meat first by boiling or baking before you place it in a dehydrator. Overall, making jerky is a three step process.

1. Marinate the meat in a refrigerator. Using a marinade or cure can tenderize and flavor the jerky before cooking and dehydrating.

2. Steam, boil or roast the meat to a temperature of 160 degrees Fahrenheit.

3. Dry the meats in a food dehydrator or through other methods that will maintain a temperature of

at least 130 to 140 degrees Fahrenheit during the entire drying process.

It is best to prefreeze your meat, so it is easier to slice into jerky. Cut partially thawed meat into long slices about 1/4 inch thick. For a more tender jerky, cut it at right angles to long muscles or across the grain. Prevent off flavors by trying to remove as much fat as possible.

The next step to consider is curing. There are a few methods of curing to consider.

CURING

There are three main ways to cure meats:

1. Dry Curing

2. Wet Curing

3. Combination Curing

DRY CURING

Dry curing meats have been around since the 13th century. It is basically the same today with the addition of nitrates. Before smoking or drying the salt with nitrates is rubbed in meat cuts. The salt dehydrates and draws the moisture out of it. The dry curing method is best for all types of sausages, bacon, and hams that are going to be air dried. After curing, most meats are smoked then air dried, and no cooking is needed.

The dry cure method is characterized by fast action and can be used in a wide range of temperature variations compared to other curing methods. The significant loss of water will result in a loss of meat weight, but the end product has a more pronounced flavor. The meat will also be better preserved. Dry curing is suitable for meats that aren't cooked but smoked and/or air-dried. It is popular among those living in hot climates with no refrigeration.

Salt Curing

People seldom salt cure meat without nitrite today. There are a few undeveloped countries where fish is still preserved with salt. There are only a few sausage and salami products that are cured with salt alone. Salt curing provides three main benefits:

1. Adds flavor

2. Prevents microbial growth

3. Increases water retention and meat/fat binding

Salt itself doesn't kill bacteria, but it will prevent and/or slow its development. In order for salt curing to be effective, it needs to be at a concentration of 10% or higher. Salt concentrations of 6% will prevent Clostridium botulinum spores from turning into toxins, but they may become active if smoked at low temperatures. You can eliminate this danger by adding sodium nitrite.

Salting causes two physical reactions: diffusion and water binding. No chemical reactions occur. Salting is the fastest curing option since it rapidly removes water from the meat. The salt migrates into the meat as the water travels to the outside surface of the meat and leaks out of it. This creates less water and more salt in the meat. Both factors are less favorable for the development of bacteria in the meat. Often the only products that are salt-cured today are those with pork back fat and some hams that are air dried for a long time.

HOW DRY CURING WORKS

To guarantee a continuous supply of salt and an uninterrupted curing process, dry curing is done in a few stages.

First, the ingredients need to be completely mixed and divided into two equal parts. The first part of the mix is rubbed into the meat. During this initial salting, it is important to completely cover all of the meat surfaces since the salt level is the only method of protection against bacteria growth.

Next, the meats need to be packed tightly into a container. Larger pieces should be placed on the bottom and smaller pieces on the top. If you have the skin on you should pack them skin side down within the container. The liquid will accumulate on the bottom of the container. If you are going to cure at low temperatures of 35-40 degrees Fahrenheit, then you can allow the liquid to stay in the container. If you are going to cure at higher temperatures, then you need to have holes in the bottom of the container for the liquid to drain off and not be re-absorbed by the meat.

The remaining part of the dry cure mixture should be divided into two parts, using each part for two additional saltings. The second cure is to be applied exactly like the first. When repacking, place the meat pieces in a different order from their original positions. Apply the third cure the same as the second.

For ideal results, you should repack meats on the twenty-first day. By reapplying the cure in stages, you will have a continuous supply of salt and nitrate that continues the process. Once curing is complete, the meat needs to be rinsed in fresh water to remove any crystallized salt that is on the surface. The meats can then be hung or placed on a wire mesh for draining. The meat should be stored at a refrigerated temperature of 38-40 degrees Fahrenheit.

There are two types of dry cures. If curing times of 14 days or less are required, then you should use Cure 1 with a standard of 1 oz cure for 25 pounds of meat. For longer curing times you can use Cure 2 which contains nitrate. For this cure you should use the following mix per 25 pounds of meat:

✓ 2 oz. cure

✓ 12 oz. canning salt

✓ 6 oz. dextrose or brown sugar

✓ Seasonings

Curing Times

The length of curing time often depends on the size of the meat and its composition. Fatty tissue and skin will create a barrier to the curing solution. For example, with ham, the curing solution begins to penetrate on the lean meat side and progresses towards the bone with very little penetration on the fatty skin side. While it seems easy enough to remove the fat simply, this may not be the best solution. The fat also acts as a barrier to smoking and removal of moisture. For larger pieces of meat, it is simply best to re-arrange the meat on the third and tenth days of curing.

The basic rule for dry curing times is two days per pound with small cuts and three days per pound for larger pieces of meat. Over curing will lead to meat that is too salty. Seasoning and spices are often applied after the last re-salting has happened.

WET CURING

The wet curing method, also known as brining, sweet pickle or immersion curing; is often used for larger cuts of meat that are later smoked. It is done by placing meats in a wet curing solution of water, salt, nitrites, and sometimes sugar. The sugar is often only added when curing at refrigerator temperatures. Otherwise, it will start to ferment and spoil the meat.

Wet curing is a traditional, time-consuming method that is often used for large hams that are submerged for up to six weeks and turned over regularly. Since there is a long curing time, the meat is in danger of spoiling in the center. During the curing process, you need to scoop up the foam and any slime that gathers on the surface since it can be a source of contamination. Smaller meat cuts often only need three to fourteen days of curing time and works well for meat that needs a shorter curing time.

With this methods, the meat needs to be turned on a daily basis, and it needs to be prevented from swimming up to the surface. Once the curing is complete, the meat should be rinsed with fresh water and placed on a wire mesh to allow draining. Even without chemicals, curing meat in this way will cause weight gain to the meat. Cured meats lead to a top quality product.

Wet curing is slower than dry curing, has a slight weight gain, produces less salty meat; but does have a shorter shelf life and a milder flavor. Today, the wet curing method is often the most popular curing option.

A wet cure can be applied in one of two ways:

1. Immersing the meat in a curing solution.

2. Spray pumping meats with needles and curing solution.

HOW WET CURING WORKS

During the wet curing process, meat products lose some of its water and soluble materials such as meat juice and minerals. However, you are gaining salt. There are two distinct phases to the wet curing process.

In the first phase, the salt migrates from the solution and into the meat. At the same time, the water migrates from inside the meat to the solution outside. The process is often very fast in the first seven days, then slows down as the salt pressure equalizes on both sides of the meat until the process stops. During this phase, there is a net meat loss as a result of water loss as well as some inevitable loss of natural juices and meat protein. This loss is far less than salting and dry curing methods.

In the second phase, the salt that is already inside the meat penetrates the muscle fibers causing them to swell, so they are able to hold water inside them. This allows the solution to flow back into the meat, creating a net gain of meat that is determined by the total curing time, the amount of water in the meat, salt concentration and method of curing. Under normal conditions, this happens after thirty days of curing.

While the exchange of salt and water stops after the salt pressure is balanced on both sides, the chemical and biological reactions continue. This results in the cured meat maturing or aging and developing a characteristic aroma that is very noticeable.

Soaking

The purpose of soaking meat is to provide even salt distribution within the meat. For example, a large piece of meat won't have uniform salt distribution even when fully cured. This is because of skin and fat layers that create a barrier to salt penetration. After curing there will be more salt near the lean area of the meat than the fat area.

When you immerse meat in a cold fresh water solution, it will cause the salt to start traveling outwards in a type of reverse curing. The outside areas and surface of the meat contain the most salt since they have the shortest distance to the water. These areas will lose salt first, causing the salt distribution to be more uniform. Soaking can be done on fully smoked and cooked sausages that are often over salted.

You can also get more uniform salt distribution by pumping meat with a brine injective and eliminate the need to soak. With this option, you are directly injecting brine under the fat layer to make the curing process more rapid.

Today, meat preservation is secondary to the taste of a product. It is best to soak meats in running water, but if this isn't possible, then you should replace the water every thirty minutes. Soaking is for the purpose of removing the excess salt that accumulates on the surface of the meats and gives a more uniform distribution of salt within the meat.

Soaking removes about 10% of the curing ingredients that you introduced to the meat. The surface of the meat needs to be washed with water to remove any salt crystals that would otherwise prevent smoke penetration. The meats are then hung or placed on wire mesh so they can drip for twenty-four hours before smoking. The meat should be stored at refrigerated temperatures of 38-40 degrees Fahrenheit.

DRAINING

Any rinsing or soaking should be done in cold running water of 62-68 degrees Fahrenheit and the time is determined by the size of the meat pieces and the total curing time. If you aren't going to soak meats after curing, then you should briefly rinse them in warm water at a temperature of 106-114 degrees Fahrenheit before hanging in a well-ventilated area for drying.

The surface of the meat needs to be dry or feel tacky before it can move on to smoking. You can speed up the drying process with an air fan or in a smoker by applying heat. The temperature should be no higher than 120 degrees Fahrenheit, and all drafts should be opened to allow for fresh air flow. This process can typically take up to a day.

PUMPING

Many commercial meat plants will add phosphates to the wet cure solution in order to hold extra amounts of water. In a small process, you can use pumping to get 80% of the curing solution into the meat. There are three main advantages to using the pumping method:

1. You can precisely introduce curing solution to the most needed areas.

2. You can shorten the curing time.

3. You can inject spices and special flavorings directly into the meat.

The total amount of solution that you introduce to the meat will depend on the total curing time:

➤ Fast curing of seven to fourteen days will require about 10-12% brine in relation to the original meat weight.

➤ Slow curing of thirty to fifty days will require about 5-6% brine in relation to the original meat weight.

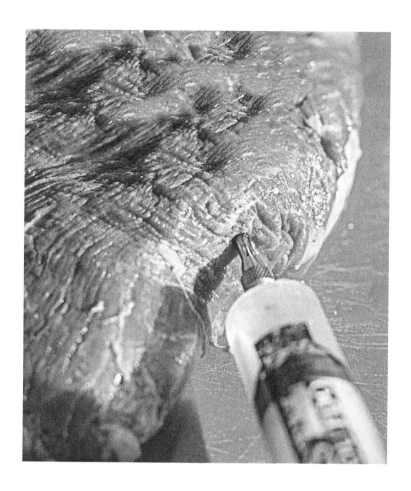

It is important to remember that pumping meat will introduce moisture into the product and this can be undesirable in dry meats or when the main purpose of curing is for preservation. In these situations, dry curing may be more suitable.

COMBINATION CURING

The first option is to combine the dry cure method with spray pumping. For larger meats, you can spray pump the curing solution inside and rub the outside with a dry mix.

Another option is to combine the wet cure method with spray pumping. This will make the curing process faster.

Combination curing is a popular option since it reduces processing time.

CURING PROBLEMS

What happens if you end up adding too much or too little cure? If you don't have enough cure, you'll experience a little loss of color as well as some loss of flavor. It has been found that a minimum of 40-50 ppm nitrite is the minimum needed for meaningful curing. If you have too much cure, it will be absorbed by the meat and ingested.

What happens if you cure too long or too short? Too short of a curing time means some parts of the meat won't have an even color. A longer curing time by a few days won't affect much as long as the meat is refrigerated. It is always a good idea to taste your meats at the end of curing. It is always possible to cure your meats longer in a heavier brine or soak them in cold water to raise or lower the salt content respectively.

BEST MEATS FOR CURING

When it comes to curing, each type of meat has its own advantages and disadvantages. Consider the best meats for curing and their advantages and disadvantages.

➢ Pork - Best for color, taste, and flavor.

➢ Beef - Loses a lot of protein and minerals.

➢ Lamb - Doesn't have a significant change.

➢ Veal - Doesn't have a significant change.

➤ Poultry - Does well all around with curing.

➤ Fish - Is greatly improved with curing.

After curing meats, they can either be ready to eat or you can further process them before getting a final product. When it comes to further processing the most common processes are smoking, fermenting and drying.

SMOKING PROCESS

Smoking is a process that helps to preserve and flavor meat. Some popular smoked meats include hams, bacon, salmon, herring, and oysters. It is important that you know the difference between smoking for preservation and smoking for texture and flavor. There are three ways that people smoke meat: hot smoking, cold smoking, and liquid smoking.

HOT SMOKING

This method is typically done in a smokehouse or a modern electric kiln. The process takes place in a short period of time, just long enough to cook the meat. The meat is often cooked using either a burning fire or the electric elements of a kiln.

COLD SMOKING

Cold smoking is a much longer process that takes twelve to twenty-four hours and is done over a smoldering fire no hotter than 85 degrees Fahrenheit. Since this puts most foods in the temperature danger range, it is possible that microbial growth occurs. As a result, this smoking method is often reserved for fermented, salted and/or cured meats. Most cold smoked products need to be cooked to an internal temperature of 160 degrees Fahrenheit before being consumed. However, smoked salmon and mackerel are the exceptions.

LIQUID SMOKING

Many manufacturers of meat products both large and small choose to use liquid smoke in order to add flavor to their food. Liquid smoke offers the benefits of being precisely controlled and providing instant flavor.

After the curing and/or smoking stages you come to the important part of drying your beef jerky. Let's take a look at what goes into this process.

DRYING PROCESS

From early times meat was dried in smoke houses with a small burning fire. Artificial drying or dehydrating started around 1795 when French inventors first designed a hot air food dehydrator. A short time later another French inventor developed the canning process. Dehydrating and canning led to new advances in food preservation.

Drying meats works on a principle of water content. Most food has a water content of 80-95% with most meats having a water content of 50-75%. After drying, most foods have 10-20% water content. There are three main types of drying you want to consider:

1. Sun drying

2. Solar drying

3. Dehydration

There is a fourth option of freeze drying, but since this is beyond the ability of most small processes, we'll only stick with the three options.

THE PRINCIPLES OF DRYING FOOD

Drying is easily defined as the process of removing water from food into the air. With solar drying, the air then escapes into the atmosphere while in a dehydrator the moist air is sucked out by a fan. In order for water to evaporate from food it needs to be heated, which requires an energy source. For solar drying, this is done through the sun, but a dehydrator relies on electricity to heat the air and move the fans. As temperature increases, the vapor pressure of the water also increases until the water molecules break free and evaporate. As the surface water leaves, it is replaced by water from within the food, thus dehydrating the food.

A successful drying process relies on two things:

1. Enough heat to remove moisture without actually cooking the food.

2. Having proper air circulation to carry away moisture.

There are also four factors that can influence the drying process:

1. The greater the surface area or the more porous the surface, the faster the food dries.

2. The faster the air flows over the food, the faster the food dries.

3. A higher air temperature means food dries faster.

4. Lower humidity means the food dries faster.

MEATS SUITABLE FOR DRYING

Meat drying is an efficient way to preserve food and is actually quite simple to do. Under ambient temperatures, you can store dried meat for many months. Since dried meat has low water content, you can prevent microbial spoilage of muscle proteins. However, drying won't stop the deterioration of adhered fatty tissue through rancidity. This is why lean meat is best for drying. This includes the following:

✓ Beef

✓ Buffalo

✓ Goat

✓ Deer

✓ Antelope

Mutton and pork are the lowest on the list since even very lean meat in these animals contains higher amounts of inter-muscular fat than other meats and is prone to oxidation and faster rancidity.

PREPARING MEAT FOR DRYING

Since drying meat is faster for a shorter distance to the center of the meat, most meat is cut into narrow strips or flat pieces before drying. The two most recommended shapes are the following:

1. Strips with a rectangular cross section of 1 x 1 cm

2. Flat or leaf shaped pieces with a cross section of 0.5 cm x 3 to 5 cm

For thick or large pieces of meat, the moisture content in the center will remain high for too long and at the high ambient temperatures of drying, microbial spoilage can easy occur. You should also make sure you carefully trim off any visible fatty tissues in order to extend the shelf life of dried meat. Now let's take a look at some of the drying methods.

SUN DRYING

For thousands of years, the primary method of drying was using the sun. A climate of warm temperatures, low humidity, and prevailing winds is ideal for sun drying. However, sun drying is only effective in an area with low to moderate humidity. These conditions are most ideal in California, Spain, and Italy. The states within the Gulf of Mexico are too humid for sun drying. In humid climates, sun drying can be slow, and mold may appear.

Sun drying has the disadvantage of being at the mercy of the elements. You can't control the weather. If wet weather occurs, you'll need to either cover your product or bring it inside. Sun drying not only requires a lot of labor, but it also requires an extensive amount of space.

You can increase space and effectiveness of sun drying by placing screens on blocks for better air flow. You can also put a sheet of aluminum under the blocks to reflect sun rays and increase the drying temperature. It is best to use screens made from stainless steel or food grade plastic. You'll also need to consider a protective cover since drying meats can attract insects and birds. The ideal covers are a second screen or a sheet of cheesecloth.

SOLAR DRYING

Solar drying is similar to sun drying in that it relies on sun energy to dry meats, but the process takes place in a solar drying designed and built for the sole purpose of drying meat. With a solar dryer, the sun enters an enclosed chamber where it hits a dark surface and converts the sun's energy to heat. The heat then dries the food. A natural draft helps with air flow, which is controlled through adjusting of the vents. The same principles are used in traditional smokehouses.

Depending on your design and construction the sun collector and drying chamber can be combined or separate. If the collector is free standing, then the heat needs to be directed into the drying chamber. You may also want to have a backup source of electric heating if you live in an area where the sun is not around for periods long enough to lack a consistent heat source.

Solar drying offers the following benefits over traditional sun drying:

➢ Faster drying

➢ Higher temperatures

➢ Better airflow and temperature control

➢ Protection from the elements

The inside of the dryer needs to be lined with black absorbing material or painted black. The cold air will flow in from the bottom, but the sun rays will heat up the drying chamber and the air. The warm air will rise and leave the chamber. This natural air flow will depend on the height or pressure between the fresh air intake and the hot air exhaust. The bigger the difference, the faster your air flow.

In the daytime, the solar dryer works with sun energy. The warming chamber provides warm air to the drying chamber that should have removable trays or other methods of storing food. For a hot or humid area that may not have significant drying during periods of the day or night you should have an optional heating element that you can turn on and continue drying.

Lastly, you'll want a pipe stack to allow the escape of warm and moist air. The higher your pipe, the faster and stronger your air flow. If you make the pipe adjustable, then the air flow and humidity can be controlled by you during the drying process. You can even choose to install a thermometer and humidity sensor for precise control.

SOLAR DRYING TECHNIQUES

Often meat drying in a solar dryer is done on trays. This not only allows a higher load, but it also makes the process less labor intensive. The trays need to be built in such a way that they can be piled on each other while allowing for sufficient air circulation. The trays are often made from wire or fiber mesh that allows for air penetration with a sturdy frame.

The best technique is to dry the meat until they reach a hard and solid texture. Often the total drying time is 48 hours. The most effective drying times are for 8 hours a day during the main solar impact.

DEHYDRATION

Modern day food processors often used food dehydrators that offer faster drying with nearly immediate removal of moisture and inhibits bacterial growth. Dehydrators work best with thinly sliced meats. However, dehydration is a more expensive option do to the electricity costs. However, it does give you the greatest control since weather changes aren't a problem. Food dehydrators fall into two categories:

1. Those with stackable trays

2. Those made from a rigid box with removable shelves

Small dehydrators don't have humidity control, and most of the drying is done in a home without high humidity. The rigid box models have a base-mounted fan that moves the hot air vertically, and some have a rear-mounted fan to move air horizontally. Still, other models have no fan and rely on convection drying.

CHOOSING A DEHYDRATOR

There are four main features you need to consider when choosing what dehydrator to purchase.

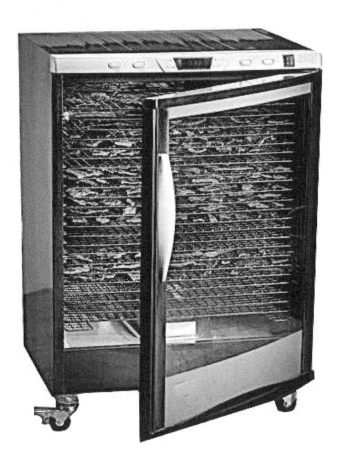

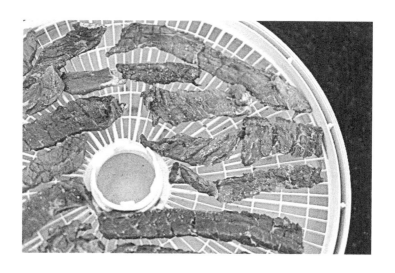

The first thing you want to consider is temperature control. You should choose a unit that allows you to set temperature by degree and not simply a low, medium or high setting. For drying meat, you want a unit that is capable of maintaining 160 degrees Fahrenheit.

Secondly, you want to get a dehydrator with a timer. However, keep in mind that a timer doesn't determine when food is dried. It doesn't matter if the timer is mechanical or digital, but a timer is important.

Then you want to consider the size based on your drying needs. Make sure you have enough counter space for your dehydrator and that it meets your production needs.

Lastly, you want to consider the accessories. Non-stick trays and mats are helpful when making jerky with honey or other sticky additives. For smaller items, you'll want a finer mesh screen.

FINISHED PRODUCT

Drying fresh and untreated meat will take at least two days and sometimes up to three or four days. After this, the meat is ready for consumption and can be packaged for sale. At this point, there are several quality criteria the meat needs to achieve.

First is the appearance of the meat. It needs to be as uniform as possible. The absence of any large wrinkles and notches means you achieved a desired steady and uniform dehydration.

Second is the color on the surface of the meat. The cross-cut should be uniform and dark red. Fast drying is seen by a darker peripheral layer and a bright red color in the center. This means certain meat parts are still susceptible to microbial growth.

The third is the texture. Properly dried meat needs to be hard and similar to frozen meat. You can recognize a softer texture by pressing the meat between your fingers. These pieces need to dry for at least one more day.

Lastly, there are the criteria of taste and flavor. Dried meat should have a mild salty taste if you don't add spices or flavoring. There should be no off odors. There may be a slightly rancid flavor, but this is typical for chemical changes that occur during drying and storage.

One thing we've discussed a lot throughout this book is microbial growth. Anytime you are working with raw meat and curing there is the potential for bacterial growth and other health concerns. So when it comes to making natural beef jerky, it is important that you take proper precautions and learn about health and safety for making jerky at home. Let's first look at the health concerns you need to be aware of.

BEEF JERKY SAFETY

Concern for food safety has become a big issue in recent years. Bacteria, yeasts, and molds can all grow on meat. Most foodborne diseases come from bacterial growth and meat results in nearly one-third of outbreaks in the United States. The pathogens that pose the greatest risk are Salmonella, Campylobacter, Escherichia, Listeria, and Toxoplasma.

As a natural beef jerky maker, you are meeting the consumer demand for minimally processed foods that are convenient to use. However, many consumers want natural products that don't contain a significant amount of salt. This can all have a huge impact on the safety of food or the process involved.

FOOD POISONING ORGANISMS

Microorganisms are commonly found in foods. Some of them can even be harmless. Others can produce chemicals that alter the acceptability of the food and cause spoilage. The following are some of the pathogenic organisms that you need to be aware of when making natural jerky.

BOTULISM

Botulism occurs from ingesting a toxin that typically results from inadequate home food processing or preservation. This bacteria requires a moist, oxygen-free environment with the low acidity of pH 4.6 or greater and a temperature danger zone of 38 to 140 degrees Fahrenheit. C. Botulinum will form heat-resistant spores that are dangerous when allowed to germinate, grow and produce toxins. The toxin is inactivated at 180 degrees Fahrenheit for four minutes. C. Botulinum grows strongest in moist foods that are low in salt.

CLOSTRIDIUM

Some spores of Clostridium can become so heat resistant that they even survive boiling for four or more hours. In addition, these spores can germinate to growing cells when cooking drives off oxygen, kills competitive organisms and heat-shocks the spores. After germination, the spores will grow in an environment that is warm, moist, and protein-rich with little or no oxygen.

LISTERIA

This bacteria is commonly found in fermented raw meat sausages, raw and cooked poultry, raw meats and raw or smoked fish. It can grow at temperatures as low as three degrees Celsius, meaning it can multiply in refrigerated foods. The organism grows best in a pH range of 5.0 to 9.5 and is even resistant to freezing. It is also salt tolerant and somewhat resistant to drying but can be easily destroyed by heating.

E. COLI

E. coli is most commonly associated with ground beef, but all manners of smoked and cured foods have been implicated in outbreaks. Some studies show that E. coli can survive standard dry fermentation processing conditions.

TRICHINOSIS

Trichinosis is an infestation of trichinae, a parasite that invades the muscles and causes severe pain and edema. It is most common in pork and certain wild game but can be avoided by cooking the meat to an internal temperature of 150 degrees Fahrenheit or more. Freezing the meat can also kill the trichinae.

STAPHYLOCOCCUS

This bacteria is more salt tolerant than others. It is also naturally present on human skin, and only some species will cause toxic food poisoning. Proper hand washing and handling can reduce the risk of bacterial growth and toxin formation. The bacteria itself is killed at temperatures of 120 degrees Fahrenheit, but the toxin itself is heat resistant, so you want to keep the organism from growing. This is done through proper food handling.

SALMONELLA

This bacteria occurs in raw meats, poultry and fish products including jerky. The bacteria thrives at temperatures between 40 and 140 degrees Fahrenheit. However, they are easily destroyed by cooking to 165 degrees Fahrenheit and won't grow at refrigerator or freezer temperatures. Although they can survive in refrigeration and freezing, so they will grow again when warmed to room temperature.

CAMPYLOBACTER

This organism primarily grows in raw chicken. It grows best in a reduced oxygen environment. It is easily killed at temperatures above 120 degrees Fahrenheit and can be inhibited by acid, salt and drying. It stops multiplying at temperatures under 85 degrees Fahrenheit.

INHIBITING PATHOGENS

Salt and nitrates or nitrites are the main chemicals that help to inhibit pathogen growth on cured meats. Along with these ingredients, pH and temperature are factors that can prohibit the growth of pathogens in meat. The following table will show you some of the extreme parameters that can cause the growth of pathogens in meat.

Pathogen	Minimum pH	Max % Salt	Min. Temp.	Oxygen Req.
Campylobacter	4.9	2	86	MA
Clostridium	4.7	10	38	AN
E. Coli	3.6	8	33	FA
Listeria	4.8	12	32	FA
Salmonella	4.0	8	41	FA
Staphylococcus	4.0	20	41	FA

All temperatures are in Fahrenheit. MA = Microaerophilic meaning it requires limited levels of oxygen. AN = Anaerobic meaning it requires the absence of oxygen. FA = Facultative anaerobic meaning it can grow either with or without oxygen.

CRITICAL PRESERVATION POINTS

The FDA has produced specific guidelines to help with the safety of food production. The following are their guidelines to help minimize the risk of exposure to the above organisms.

SANITATION

Both before and after working you should make sure that all equipment, work surfaces, and utensils are cleaned and sanitized. In a home operation, a good option for sanitizing is to use one tablespoon of chlorine bleach in a gallon of warm water. Your primary focus should be on avoiding cross contamination between raw and/or dirty surfaces with clean and cooked meat.

STORAGE AND REFRIGERATION

During both refrigeration and storage your primary focus should be on keeping raw and cooked products separate. Raw products should never be stored above or in contact with any cooked products. It is a good idea to place any raw products into a pan about one to two inches deep in order to prevent meat juices from contacting other surfaces.

TEMPERATURE

As we've discussed, the danger zone for microbial growth is between 40 and 140 degrees Fahrenheit. This means you need to store, age, and cure or preserve meats in a refrigeration that is below 40 degrees Fahrenheit. Then you need to cook the meats to an internal temperature of 160 degrees Fahrenheit in order to destroy any bacteria. The appropriate recipes to follow are those that minimize preservation time and cook to a safe internal temperature, so you minimize the risk of food-related illnesses.

CURING SAFETY

MEATS

Before applying any preservation method, you want to make sure meats are fresh. Never rely on curing to salvage meat that has bacterial growth or spoilage. Some meat, especially game meat, doesn't need to be aged since it will be tenderized during the curing/smoking process. If you want to age meats, then make sure you do so well below the 40 degrees Fahrenheit danger zone.

SALT

When curing you should only use food grade salt that doesn't have any additives such as iodine. If you use salt with impurities, then you can have less desirable results, especially when curing fish. As you thaw meats, you will want to monitor and control the process to make sure it is thorough and doesn't fall outside temperature guidelines. Meat that isn't thawed properly can cause inadequate cure penetration and not following temperature guidelines can lead to spoilage or bacterial growth.

CURING COMPOUNDS

It is best to use commercially prepared cure mixes or if making your own to follow instructions carefully. If you are making them at home, it is important that you make sure you have an accurate scale. For dry-cured products that are not to be cooked, you should use a cure mixture that contains nitrate.

All meats that require cooking, smoking or canning should use a cure mixture containing nitrites. Nitrites are toxic if used in quantities higher than recommended so be very care in how you store and use them. Also, if you accidentally use nitrite instead of nitrate you'll have a lethal dose of nitrite in the final cured product. This is why it can be safer to use commercially prepared mixes.

CURE PENETRATION

Cure mixtures won't work with frozen meats. Before you cure, it is important that you thaw meats in the refrigerator completely. For jerky purposes, the meat should be prepared to uniform sizes, so there is even cure penetration. This is especially important during dry and immersion curing. All meat surfaces need to be rotated and rubbed at intervals to sufficiently penetrate the cure during a dry curing method. Immersion curing will require periodic mixing of the batch.

Make sure curing is done at a temperature between 35-40 degrees Fahrenheit. The lower temperature helps ensure cure penetration while the upper temperature limits microbial growth. Curing solutions need to be discarded after use unless they are used in the same batch for the entire curing process because you don't want to risk cross contamination through reuse.

SMOKING SAFETY

If you have a smokehouse, make sure it works as intended for heat, airflow and moisture control. Thermometers should be appropriately calibrated and used only for internal meat temperatures. Develop and use procedures that ensure appropriate thermal treatment of cooking meats. If you are going to smoke meats for a long period of time within the danger zone of 40 to 140 degrees Fahrenheit, then your meat should be salted or cured first.

SMOKE COOKING

If you are going to smoke cook food, you need to have them reach an appropriate internal temperature as listed by the USDA in the following table:

Product	Temperature - Degrees

	Fahrenheit
Ground turkey or chicken	165
Ground veal, beef, lamb or pork	160
Medium rare fresh beef	145
Medium fresh beef	160
Well done beef	170
Medium rare veal	145
Medium veal	160

Well done veal	170
Medium-rare lamb	145
Medium lamb	160
Well done lamb	170
Medium pork	160
Well done pork	170
Whole chicken	180
Whole turkey	180
Roasted poultry breasts	170
Poultry thighs	180

and wings	
Stuffing	165
Duck and Goose	180
Fresh or raw ham	160
Pre-cooked or reheating ham	140
Fin fish	Until opaque and flakes easily
Shrimp, lobster or crab	Red and flesh pearly opaque
Scallops	Milky white or opaque and firm

Clams, mussels or oysters	Until shell opens

COOLING

After cooking products should be rapidly cooled to below 40 degrees Fahrenheit and kept refrigerated. Cooked fish products need to be cooled to below 70 degrees Fahrenheit within two hours and then to below 40 degrees Fahrenheit within four hours. You should reduce your handling of any cooked products.

STORAGE

Cured or smoked poultry should be stored in the refrigerator no longer than two weeks and in the freezer no longer than one year. Lightly cured fish can be stored in the refrigerator for 10 to 14 days or in the freezer for 2-3 months. Vacuum packaged meats still need to be kept at 40 degrees

Fahrenheit, since the reduce oxygen atmosphere can cause botulism poisoning.

STARTING A JERKY BUSINESS

Starting a jerky business can be simply making small batches at home to sell at the local market or a larger operation. Either way, a jerky business is similar to other food businesses; the art of making the food is easy, but the process of getting your business started can be a bit of a challenge. However, don't let this discourage you; there are over 500 successful jerky brands in the United States, and you can be one of them. Let's first consider the equipment you need to get started.

EQUIPMENT YOU WILL NEED

DEHYDRATOR

Depending on your location, regulations may require you to get a commercial National Safety Foundation (NSF) certified dehydrator. These can potentially cost $10,000; so make sure you check regulations in your area. If possible, you can get a used dehydrator and save a lot of money. Look in classifieds focused on the restaurant industry, and you may find a company going out of business that you can get one for 1/2 to 1/4 of the original price.

FOOD SLICER

Another big piece of equipment you'll need is a commercial food slicer. Depending on the size, these can cost $750 or more. Again, you can save money by finding a used one.

PACKAGING

You shouldn't have to spend too much on bags since you don't need anything too elaborate. Just buy some resealable bags in bulk. Buying in larger amounts will save you money.

For simple custom labels, you'll want to consider getting a label maker and create your own template. The initial cost can be as high as $10,000 in labeling costs, but it can get cheaper over time. However, you can research and determine what labeling methods work for you and potentially find something a little cheaper.

OXYGEN ABSORBERS

These aren't a mandatory supply, but they can be helpful. When used properly they are powerful and not very expensive. You can often buy them in bulk of 500 or more. However, once you open the package you'll need to use them within days, or they will no longer be useful; no matter how much you keep them sealed from the air.

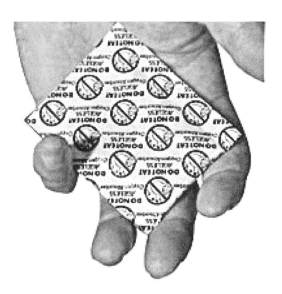

Once you have the equipment, you need to start focusing on the business aspect of starting a jerky business. The first thing you need to do is make sure you are aware of all the regulations.

SETTING UP YOUR BUSINESS

INCORPORATING YOUR BUSINESS

When you choose a legal entity for your jerky business there are two main factors to consider:

4. What you want the business structure to be

5. The type of business model you intend to build

Often you have the option of choosing to file as a limited liability company or LLC, general partnership or even sole proprietorship. A sole proprietorship is the ideal business structure for someone starting a home-based business, especially if it is a moderate start from you home. However, most prefer the benefits of a Limited Liability Company or LLC.

If you plan to eventually expand your Jerky business online or expand beyond your area to few neighboring states or even national, then you definitely don't want to file as a sole proprietor. In this instance, you should definitely file as an LLC.

When you file as an LLC, you will be able to protect yourself from personal liability. This means that if anything goes wrong while operating your business then only the money you invested into the company is at risk. This isn't the case if you file as a sole proprietor or a general partnership. LLCs are simple and flexible to operate since you won't need a board of directors, shareholder meetings or other managerial formalities in order to run your business.

Here are all the legal business structures you can choose from, it is best to get some advice from your CPA/accountant or an attorney.

BUSINESS STRUCTURE

When starting a business, there are five different business structures you can choose from:

❖ Sole Proprietor

❖ Partnership

❖ Corporation (Inc. or Ltd.)

❖ S Corporation

❖ Limited Liability Company (LLC)

SOLE PROPRIETOR

This is not the safest structure for any food related business. It is used for a business owned by a single person or a married couple. Under this structure, the owner is personally liable for all business debts and may file on their personal income tax.

PARTNERSHIP

This is another inexpensive business structure to form. It often requires an agreement between two or more individuals who are going to jointly own and operate a business.

The partners will share all aspects of the business in accordance with the agreement. Partnerships don't pay taxes, but they need to file an informational return. Individual partners then report their share of profits and losses on their personal tax returns.

CORPORATION (INC. OR LTD.)

This is one of the more complex business structures and has the most startup costs of any business structure. It isn't a very common structure among small businesses since there are shares of stocks involved.

Profits are taxed both at the corporate level and again when distributed to shareholders. When you structure a business at this level, there are often lawyers involved.

S CORPORATION

This is one of the most popular types of business entity people forms to it avoid double taxation. It is taxed similarly to a partnership entity. But an S Corp. needs to be approved to be classified as such, so it isn't very common among cleaning businesses.

LIMITED LIABILITY COMPANY (LLC)

This is the most common business structure among auto dealership businesses. It offers benefits for small businesses since it reduces the risk of losing all your personal assets in case you are faced with a lawsuit. It provides a clear separation between business and personal assets. You can also elect to be taxed as a corporation, which saves you money come tax time.

If you are unsure which specific business structure you should choose then, you can discuss it with an accountant. They will direct you in the best possible option for what your business goals are.

Here is a sample article of incorporation for an LLC entity.

STATE OF ALABAMA:

COUNTY OF BALDWIN:

ARTICLES OF ORGANIZATION

OF

ALL NATURAL JERKY LLC

The undersigned, acting as organizers of the All Natural Jerky LLC under the Alabama Limited

Liability Company Act, adopt the following Articles of Organization for said Limited Liability Company.

Article I

Name of the Company

The name of the limited liability company is All Natural Jerky LLC (the "Company").

Article II

Period of Duration

The period of duration is ninety (90) years from the date of filing of these Articles of Organization with the Alabama Secretary of State unless the Company is sooner dissolved.

Article III

Purpose of the Company

The Company is organized to engage in all legal and lawful purpose of producing and selling dried meat business.

Article IV

Registered Office and Agent

The Company's registered office is at address is 123 Main Court, Daphne, Alabama 36561; and the name and the address of the Company's initial registered agent is John Doe, 123 Main Court, Daphne, Alabama 36561

Article V

Members of the Organization

There is one (1) member, all of which are identified in the Exhibit A attached hereto and a part hereof. The initial capital contribution agreed to be made by both members are also listed on Exhibit A. The members have not agreed to make any additional contributions, but may agree to do so in the future upon the terms and conditions as set forth in the Operating Agreement.

Article VI

Additional Members

The members, as identified in the Company's Operating Agreement, reserve the right to admit additional members and determine the Capital Contributions of such Members. Notwithstanding the foregoing, the additional Members may not become managing unless and until selected to such position as provided in Article VII of the Company's Operating Agreement.

Article VII

Contribution upon Withdrawal of Members

The members shall have the right to continue the company upon the death, retirement, resignation, expulsion, bankruptcy or dissolution of a member or occurrence of any event which terminates the continued membership of a member in the Company (collectively, "Withdrawal"), as long as there is at least One remaining member, and the remaining member agree to continue the Company by unanimous written consent within 90 days after the Withdrawal of a Member, as set forth in the Operating Agreement of the Company.

Article VIII

Manager

The name and business address of the initial manager is:

John Doe

All Natural Jerky LLC

123 Main Court

Daphne, Alabama 36561

The manager may be removed and replaced by the Members as provided in the Operating Agreement.

IN WITNESS WHEREOF, the undersigned have caused these Articles of Organization to be executed this ……………. Day of ……………………. 2010

_____

_____

All Natural Jerky LLC

DATE

AN ALABAMA CORPORATION

BY: John Doe

ITS: Managing Member

This instrument prepared by:

Jane Doe

999 Super Ct

Daphne, Al 36561

EXHIBIT A

MEMBERS CONTRIBUTION	INTIAL INTEREST

John Doe   Future Services

Rendered   100%

EIN NUMBER FROM IRS

EIN or Employer Identification number is essentially a social security or tax identification number but for your business. IRS and many other governmental agencies can identify your business via this unique 9 digit number.

Remember you will not need this number if you choose to be a sole proprietorship for your business.

It is simple to apply, either you can do it yourself or get your accountant to do it for you, but the process is simple, you fill out the form SS-4, which can be filed online, via Fax or via mail.

Here is a link to IRS website where you can download or fill out the form online.

Form SS-4
(Rev. January 2010)
Department of the Treasury
Internal Revenue Service

Application for Employer Identification Number

(For use by employers, corporations, partnerships, trusts, estates, churches, government agencies, Indian tribal entities, certain individuals, and others.)

► See separate instructions for each line. ► Keep a copy for your records.

OMB No. 1545-0003

EIN

1	Legal name of entity (or individual) for whom the EIN is being requested

Type or print clearly.

2	Trade name of business (if different from name on line 1)	3	Executor, administrator, trustee, "care of" name

4a	Mailing address (room, apt., suite no. and street, or P.O. box)	5a	Street address (if different) (Do not enter a P.O. box.)
4b	City, state, and ZIP code (if foreign, see instructions)	5b	City, state, and ZIP code (if foreign, see instructions)

6	County and state where principal business is located

7a	Name of responsible party	7b	SSN, ITIN, or EIN

8a	Is this application for a limited liability company (LLC) (or a foreign equivalent)? ☐ Yes ☐ No	8b	If 8a is "Yes," enter the number of LLC members ►

8c If 8a is "Yes," was the LLC organized in the United States? . . . . ☐ Yes ☐ No

9a Type of entity (check only one box). Caution. If 8a is "Yes," see the instructions for the correct box to check.

☐ Sole proprietor (SSN) _____
☐ Partnership
☐ Corporation (enter form number to be filed) ► _____
☐ Personal service corporation
☐ Church or church-controlled organization
☐ Other nonprofit organization (specify) ► _____
☐ Other (specify) ►

☐ Estate (SSN of decedent)
☐ Plan administrator (TIN)
☐ Trust (TIN of grantor)
☐ National Guard ☐ State/local government
☐ Farmers' cooperative ☐ Federal government/military
☐ REMIC ☐ Indian tribal governments/enterprises
Group Exemption Number (GEN) if any ►

9b	If a corporation, name the state or foreign country (if applicable) where incorporated	State		Foreign country

10 Reason for applying (check only one box)
☐ Started new business (specify type) ► _____
☐ Hired employees (Check the box and see line 13.)
☐ Compliance with IRS withholding regulations
☐ Other (specify) ►

☐ Banking purpose (specify purpose) ► _____
☐ Changed type of organization (specify new type) ► _____
☐ Purchased going business
☐ Created a trust (specify type) ► _____
☐ Created a pension plan (specify type) ► _____

11	Date business started or acquired (month, day, year). See instructions.	12	Closing month of accounting year
13	Highest number of employees expected in the next 12 months (enter -0- if none). If no employees expected, skip line 14.	14	If you expect your employment tax liability to be $1,000 or less in a full calendar year and want to file Form 944 annually instead of Forms 941 quarterly, check here. (Your employment tax liability generally will be $1,000 or less if you expect to pay $4,000 or less in total wages.) If you do not check this box, you must file Form 941 for every quarter. ☐

Agricultural	Household	Other

15 First date wages or annuities were paid (month, day, year). Note. If applicant is a withholding agent, enter date income will first be paid to nonresident alien (month, day, year) . . . . ►

16 Check one box that best describes the principal activity of your business. ☐ Health care & social assistance ☐ Wholesale-agent/broker
☐ Construction ☐ Rental & leasing ☐ Transportation & warehousing ☐ Accommodation & food service ☐ Wholesale-other ☐ Retail
☐ Real estate ☐ Manufacturing ☐ Finance & insurance ☐ Other (specify) ►

17 Indicate principal line of merchandise sold, specific construction work done, products produced, or services provided.

18 Has the applicant entity shown on line 1 ever applied for and received an EIN? ☐ Yes ☐ No
If "Yes," write previous EIN here ►

Third Party Designee	Complete this section only if you want to authorize the named individual to receive the entity's EIN and answer questions about the completion of this form.	
	Designee's name	Designee's telephone number (include area code)
	Address and ZIP code	Designee's fax number (include area code)

Under penalties of perjury, I declare that I have examined this application, and to the best of my knowledge and belief, it is true, correct, and complete.

Name and title (type or print clearly) ►

Applicant's telephone number (include area code)

Applicant's fax number (include area code)

OPENING A COMMERCIAL BANK ACCOUNT

This is one important step, but it can only be done after you have a fully executed article of incorporation which has been approved by the state, and you have an EIN number assigned by the IRS.

Once you have these two documents, you should be able to go to a bank and open your first commercial bank account.

But remember to check and understand various types of commercial checking account fees, you want to find a bank that offers free or almost free commercial checking account because some larger banks can charge you hundreds of dollars each month depending on how many transactions you do. Make sure to ask and shop around before you sign on the dotted line.

6 MUST DO'S

As I've said, getting started with jerky making business is easy and doesn't require much. However, I've learned from experience and from talking to others in the industry that there are four specific things you need to do to get your business off to a good start.

NAME YOUR BUSINESS

You need to get customers to distinguish your product from others in the same industry. This means you are going to need a business name; and not just any name. You want a short name that is easy to remember while also being catchy.

You need to make sure the name you choose isn't being used by any other company. If you want to know about business names you need to contact the Patent and Trade Mark Office.

One good way to search is by searching the name you picked on Google to see if anyone else is using it for the same purpose. My advice is if you find a good name, go ahead and buy the domain name of the name you just picked, this way in future if you ever want to grow, you can have a website under that name.

You can go to Godaddy.com, name.com or any other domain name seller's site and just type the name you picked; they will tell you if that name is available for purchase with.com or .net. Typically most domain names cost around $10/year which in my opinion is a great investment.

LICENSE YOUR BUSINESS

All businesses need proper licenses to operate. This shows that you are running a legal business. However, before you are allowed to license a business, you need to determine a structure for your business. If you know an accountant or an attorney, ask them to file a legal business entity (Like an LLC, S Corp or LLP) on your behalf, this way you are legally protected from most business liabilities.

You can also go on websites like leaglzoom.com and have them draw up the document for less than what an attorney would charge you to do the same.

Once you file you file the article to incorporate your business, next step is to get an accountant or CPA to file and obtain an EIN(Employer's Identification Number) from IRS. This is similar to social security number but for business. Once you have these two documents, you can then open a commercial bank account at any local bank.

Next step would be to go to your local city office and find out what type of business and regulatory licenses you are required to have. It should take a day or two to get your licenses and permits in place, and then you are finally and officially in business.

Once you have a business license and a trademark name, customers will trust your products and be more likely to buy them.

DO A THOROUGH COMPETITIVE ANALYSIS

This is key to having a successful business. When you have a competitive analysis, you know your business's current position within the jerky making industry.

The competitive analysis allows you to get the information you need on your competitors, market share, market strategies, growth and other important factors. When you have all this information, you will be able to change or improve your business in key areas so you can increase profits and sales.

Here is a simple way you can do a competitive analysis. On a piece of paper write down the following:

1. Number of local competitors you have
2. What is their niche/what type of jerky do they sell
3. Where they sell
4. What is their pricing strategy

Once you have that list, take a look and see where you would fit in that list, how can you stand out from the crowd, what can you do differently that would make customers pay attention to your products.

In my business experience, I believe there are three ways you can always stand above the crowd. I always have tried to stand above the crowd by trying of these three strategies.

1. By making superior products than my competitors make
2. By offering 100% customer satisfaction guarantee
3. By creative pricing strategy

Let me explain what I mean by creative pricing strategy.

COME UP WITH A CREATIVE PRICING STRATEGY

Pricing is the most important factor of your business. A carefully thought out pricing strategy can make you very successful but a pricing strategy that places you above your market can literality put you out of business and on the other hand pricing below the market can wipe your bottom line profit completely clean, and before you know it, you are out of business and in debt.

That was the risky part; now the tricky part is if you stay with the market, then you are standing out in the crowd instead you are standing in the crowd. To make yourself more visible and unique and to stand tall among other competitors, you have to be really very creative when it comes to your pricing strategy, and that is where the tricky part comes is. My goal is to teach you how to implement a carefully thought out pricing strategy that can make you stand out and make you successful.

Here are few ideas I often try:

1. Always run one special where you offer discount on one particular type of jerky each month, but never the same type every month

2. Run BOGO (Buy One Get One Free) promotion every few months on select jerky (usually the ones that are not selling fast)
3. Never try to be the low price leader (It is a slippery slope, don't try to reduce your price just to stay competitive)
4. Run various package promotion during holidays (I usually make baskets with few top selling jerky, some good quality crackers, two different kinds of cheese and a bottle of chutney of some sort, all nicely wrapped)

Remember, when it comes to pricing or marketing ideas, there is no "one size fits all," not every idea works for everyone. Some strategies may work better for you than others and vice versa. So, it is a good idea to test each idea separately and document the results then analyze and see which one worked the best.

UNDERSTANDING PENNY PROFIT, PROFIT MARGIN, AND MARKUP

In business these are the three most common terms we hear every day, but what do they all mean and how they are different from each other, is a question many of you have. I know this because I get asked about this very topic time to time.

Okay let's break them down and see what they are:

PENNY PROFIT

Penny profit is essentially the actual cash profit you make by selling any items in your store. For example, say you just sold a bottle of 20 oz. Coke $1.75, what is the penny profit of that sale? To find the answer first, we need to see how much you paid to buy that bottle of Coke. Looking at your invoice from Coke shows you paid $1.00 for that bottle of coke and you sold it for $1.75. So your penny profit is $1.75-1.00 = 75 cents. Penny profit is the difference between the selling price- actual costs.

PROFIT MARGIN

Profit margin the term most widely used and understood in most every business as it is what we all use to figure out if we are making enough profit from our businesses by selling the products and services.

Profit margin is essentially the percentage of profit you make or earn when you sell a product. Confusing? Let's take a look at the same example of that bottle of coke we just used earlier.

We already know the penny profit from that sale was 75 cents. Now the profit margin is done little differently, to find out the exact margin we will have to take the penny profit and divide that number by the selling price. So it will be $1.75-$1.00=0.75, then we divide that penny profit by the selling price 0.75/$1.75 = 43% profit margin.

MARKUP

The markup, on the other hand, is somewhat similar to profit margin, but instead of dividing the penny profit by the selling price you would have to divide the penny profit by the actual cost. Let's take a look at the same example once again.

Remember our penny profit from that bottle ok Coke? It was 75 cents; now we just need to divide that by the actual cost which was a $1.00 right? Let's do this, 0.75/$1.00 = 75% Markup for that same bottle of Coke.

Let's now look at another example so you will get a clear picture between the penny profits, profit margin, and markup as they can be confusing at times.

Another Example:

Let's say you bought a candy bar for a $1.00 and sold it for $2.00

Penny profit is Selling price – Cost = Penny profit. $2.00-$1.00=$1.00

Profit Margin is Penny profit/selling price = Profit margin. $1.00/$2.00=50% profit margin

Markup is Penny profit/Cost=Penny profit.

$1.00/41.00=100% markup

In this case, you can see the profit margin is only 50% when the markup is 100% which is double in this scenario.

Remember to use Profit margin when calculating your business profit margin and not to use markup.

Here are some examples of profit margin vs. markup.

20% Markup = 16.7% Gross Profit

25% Markup = 20.0% Gross Profit

33.3% Markup = 25.0% Gross Profit

40% Markup = 28.6% Gross Profit

50% Markup = 33.0% Gross Profit

75% Markup = 42.9% Gross Profit

100% Markup = 50.0% Gross Profit

DO A REALISTIC BUSINESS FORECASTING

This is another valuable business tool if you want to have a profitable business. Business forecasting is essential to determining sales targets. A month-by-month sales forecast helps you to identify problems and opportunities. An accurate sales forecast along with a well-structured sales plan will help you to have an effective business.

These are four essential things you need to have for a successful jerky making business. In addition, I've put together five of the most common mistakes new owners in the jerky making industry make that have a significant impact on the success of their business. Here is what you need to avoid.

5 BUSINESS MISTAKES TO AVOID

It is just as important to learn from other's mistakes and know what to avoid when starting a jerky making business. Consider five of the most common mistakes new business owners make.

GETTING STARTED WITH NO EXPERIENCE

As with any small business, it is important that you have at least have some experience before you get started. This means at least having experience doing it as a hobby. If you don't have any experience, take the time to take a class or read a book such as this then practice for a while to see if you are getting good at it. If you try to start a business with no experience than you are going to be taking a greater risk than you need to.

NO RESEARCH AND BUSINESS PLAN

A solid business plan built on lots of research is essential to any business success. Making jerky as a hobby and selling a few is just a start, to turn it into a business you need to do some careful planning. You need to research bulk supplies and other business aspects.

You need to choose a name and register your business. There are a number of practical steps you need to take to start your business and having a thoroughly researched business plan will make sure you don't miss any of them.

NOT HAVING A PROPER WORKSPACE

If you are going to start a business from your home, you need to make sure you have the appropriate workspace available to accommodate the size of business you plan on running.

The more room you have and the better organized you will be, and that would also mean your business will be more efficient and productive.

NOT FINDING A NICHE

If you are going to start a jerky making business, you need to have a niche. If there is a particular type of jerky you enjoy making and you're efficient in producing them, then you should place your focus on there. There are a number of jerky options, but you want to find one that not only sells well; but will also be easy for you to mass produce.

NOT HAVING A TARGET MARKET

It is important that you know where and how you plan to sell your jerky once you get your business started. Many jerky makers choose to use a website as a way to market and sell products, but there are many other options as we discussed earlier that you should consider.

CREATIVE PACKAGING PROPER LABELING PROCESS

Once you have done all the hard work of creating some great jerky recipes, making jerky and marketing them; you don't want to waste all your hard work by falling short with a mediocre packaging.

Packaging is important, possibly just as important as the quality of your jerky. The packaging is what sells it. Hiring a good designer is essential for this step, one recommendation is trying 99deisgns.com where you can post your job description and let hundreds of designers submit samples designs, then just pick the one you like the best. The cost is reasonable too.

Next is labeling, which you will need to have to satisfy all the local, federal and state food safety and nutrition laws. This part can be done by sending each sample to a local food testing lab.

REGULATIONS

Nearly every state in the United States and province in Canada have their own rules on how jerky needs to be manufactured. Depending on where you live, there can be over 100 different rules you need to follow just to meet the minimum standards. This is why it is important to research the regulations in your area. Once you know the regulations, you can prepare your company for inspection.

INSPECTION

Depending on where you intend to sell your jerky, you may need to submit it to the government to be further processed. This is why you'll see a stamp on most jerky bags that says it was inspected by the Department of Agriculture. By law, if you are making jerky to sell you need to have your production facility inspected either state or federally.

Getting the initial inspection isn't that difficult, but maintaining it can be a bit more of a challenge. A county, state or federal health inspector can visit your production facility every day. However, an inspection may not be that big of an issue unless a consumer is going to get sick and file a complaint.

Some people choose to get around these inspection requirements by hiring an inspected and approved meat processing facility to make their jerky. The facility can make the jerky according to your recipes and even source the meat according to your requirements. You then simply need to put your label on the packaging. You'll likely need to try several facilities until you find one that makes jerky of a consistency similar to what you make at home.

GOING NATURAL (THE POPULAR NICHE)

One thing you want to consider when making jerky is whether or not you want to go natural. Many consumers today are shying away from foods that contain preservatives, artificial flavors, and fillers. Sodium nitrite is a very common preservative in jerky.

While striving to be natural, you also need to make sure you jerky can sit on a shelf for a few months and still be fresh. This means you need a preservative. Some distributors and retailers won't even stock jerky that doesn't guarantee freshness beyond a few weeks. If you want to go completely natural and have no preservatives, then you need to find a market that doesn't require a long shelf life. This could be the local farmers market, street fairs, and trade shows. Another option is to sell the jerky from home using online sources.

WHERE TO SELL

When it comes to selling your jerky, you have several options to choose from. When you first start out, you may want to limit yourself from selling to family and friends.

If you don't want to sell to them, consider at least giving away some samples and asking people you know to test your products. This allows you to get clear and honest feedback on your products before you try to sell them to the general public.

RETAIL SALES

There are plenty of retail sales channels to consider. The most popular options are local food fair/shows, farmer's markets, and the internet. You can also get good exposure for your products by using corporate venues. Look for ways to effectively build your brand by educating customers, making sales, networking and referring businesses over time.

When it comes to retail sales, you need attractive displays, set prices, business cards or flyers; anything that can spread your business information. You should also be ready to educate your customer, don't just assume they know the benefits and taste of all natural meat jerky.

One of the best ways to have success with retail sales is to meet your customers one-on-one. Take an interest in your customers and keep the focus on them and their individual needs. This way you can show them specifically how your product taste, a taste test is the best way to prove your point.

For retail sales, you should offer quantity pricing such as $6 each or four for $20 (just an example).

It is also a good idea to make sure you accept credit cards. Nearly twenty percent of sales at retail shows are from credit cards, so you would lose out on a lot of money if you don't accept credit cards. You also want to remember to collect the appropriate sales and use tax for the state you are in at the moment of sale.

ONLINE

In today's electronic focused society, perhaps the best option is to have an online presence. Having a website will allow you to appear on search engines and get attention from potential customers around the world who otherwise may not get a chance to find out about your jerky.

If you are going to set up an online presence, the first thing you need to do is find a web host and create an account. For more professionalism, you should consider purchasing your own domain name before building your website (as I mentioned earlier).

Even without HTML knowledge, you can still create a decent website with the templates most web hosts offer, or you can hire a freelancer designer to put one together for you.

Once you have your website up, you should make sure you provide information on the jerky you offer and include a portfolio of your total product line so people can get a good idea of what you have to offer. Then you'll be ready to set up for accepting online sales. Here are few online freelance hire sites you can hire from:

99designs.com

Fiverr.com

Freelancer.com

Guru.com

Upwork.com

WHOLESALE

When it comes to wholesaling, there is more than I can fit into this book. However, it is safe to say the majority of wholesaling comes from first-hand experience. There are a few key points I want to tell you about to get you started on successful wholesaling for your products.

The key is to make sure you do your homework and be prepared. Visit your potential wholesale account first and envision your jerky on their shelf. Call ahead and arrange a time to meet with the buyer at the store. Be gracious and understand what the buyer is going through; put yourself in their shoes. Don't simply drop in unannounced and expect them to hear your entire pitch.

You also want to make sure you understand wholesale pricing and terms. After you know this, design and print out copies of your products to hand out to interested parties. Wholesaling information should include a minimum opening order. This will immediately reduce your option to serious buyers only.

Also, keep in mind that you want retailers to carry a good selection of your products, so your jerky doesn't become lost on the shelf. A good wholesale opening order is about $300-$1000 or higher.

Your wholesale sell sheet should include pictures of your products with wholesale pricing next to each picture. Keep in mind that wholesale price is usually half of retail price. You should also have a minimum order for each product. Try to make your wholesale information sheet with glossy paper printed in high resolution and in full color.

These are the two main sales channels for your jerky. However, there is a lot more that goes into selling jerky than simply choosing retail and wholesale channels.

MARKETING AND PROMOTION

Organic and natural jerky products already have a good following. You've likely already done your market research to identify prospective customers. However, there are four main and proven marketing strategies that will help you increase your jerky sales.

BRAND STRATEGY

The first thing is to build a brand for your natural jerky. Remember that your brand is essentially a promise to your customer, so think carefully about the promised message you are sending to customers.

Reflect what your brand has to offer over other products on all communications including advertising, packaging, and point-of-sale displays.

Your brand promise needs to resonate with customers. Don't waste your efforts marketing to people who aren't concerned about natural ingredients.

DIRECT MAIL STRATEGY

This is the best strategy to help strengthen relationships and prompt an action from customers; whether it be going to your website or visiting a store that stocks your products.

Target residents within a specific geographic location so you can keep your costs down compared to mass mailings. This option also allows you to get creative, which makes a direct mail strategy more effective and less likely to get thrown in the garbage.

PARTNERSHIP STRATEGY

Once you have done your market research, you'll have the right information about your target audience. This will tell you about people's habits.

You can then visit establishments most likely to be frequented by your target audience and suggest a partnership arrangement. If they display and sell your jerky, you will, in turn, help them sell some of their products. There are quite a few possibilities when it comes to this option.

COMMUNITY OUTREACH

An inexpensive way to market your jerky is to get known in the community. It will only take you some time and a few free samples. Offer to speak at events that fit your target demographics. Talk about how you started your business, the jerky making process or anything that may be of interest to your target audience.

Provide samples of your jerky and ask for them to request your brand at their local retail stores. If a store knows there is a demand, then they are likely to approach you about carrying your product.

ATTENDING TRADE SHOWS

Here are few food trade shows that are the most helpful for any new food company trying to make it big in the market.

Sweet and Snack Expo

http://sweetsandsnacks.com/

Natural Products Expo West

http://www.expowest.com/ew18/Public/Enter.aspx

New England Food Show

https://nefs.restaurant.org/Home

Institute of Food Technologists Annual Meeting & Food Expo (IFT)

https://www.ift.org/

Northwest Foodservice Show

http://www.nwfoodserviceshow.com/

Summer Fancy Food Show

https://www.specialtyfood.com/shows-events/summer-fancy-food-show/

You can visit this web page below to see all the upcoming food shows around the country

https://www.deluxe.com/blog/this-food-and-beverage-trade-show-roundup-is-making-us-hungry/

LAST WORDS

So there you have it. Everything you need to know about jerky making and to get your business up and running. A little overwhelmed and not sure where to start? How about taking the time to experiment with some recipes. Consider the recipes I shared in this book to get you started and then experiment with you own ingredients based on flavor preference. To grow big, to stand out in the market, you have to come up with your own unique "secret sauce" so to speak. So, in this book my goal was to show you the inner workings of jerky making, so your creative side comes out and eventually with enough practice, you will be able to create something that is totally unique and has your name on it

After a few initial trials, once you master how to make jerky then it is time for you to come up with a solid and precise business plan. No, I am not asking you to write a 20-page business plan but a plan that you outlines your process and goals. A plan where you figure out which directions you want to go at, and for that these are the 5 following things you have decide first:

1. Would you start with natural or organic jerky or both (I recommend starting with Natural only)
2. What type of jerky will you be making (come up with at least 4-6 varieties)
3. What packaging will you have for your jerky
4. Where and how you will market your jerky
5. What pricing should you have for your jerky

Remember to start small and scale up your business as you see your sales grow. Don't invest a lot of money at the beginning buying a lot of equipment and supplies. Keep your focus on the quality and marketing side of your business, and you will see success sooner than later.

Hopefully, in this book, I was able to give you a good general overview of making jerky and starting your own business. Now get out there and start making some jerky. And be successful, remember we only live once, so why not try to be the best you can be and see where that may take you.

I want to thank you for buying my book; I am neither a professional writer nor an author, but rather a person who always had the passion for making Jerky from various type of meat products. In this book, I wanted to share my knowledge with you, as I know there are many people who share the same passion and drive as I do. So, this book is entirely dedicated to you.

Despite my best effort to make this book error free, if you happen to find any errors, I want to ask for your forgiveness ahead of time.

Just remember, my writing skills may not be best, but the knowledge I share here is pure and honest.

If you thought I added some value and shared some valuable information that you can use, please take a minute and post a review on wherever you bought this book from. This will mean the world to me. Thank you so much!!

A Gift For You

If you need a few more beef jerky recipes, feel free to email me at JimTheJerkyGuy@gmail.com

I will email you 10 of my favorite and best-selling beef jerky recipes.

Thank you!

RECIPES

Low Sodium and Carb Beef Jerky

Ingredients:

- ✓ 3 pounds beef

- ✓ 1/2 cup water

- ✓ 3 dashes liquid smoke

- ✓ 1 teaspoon pepper

- ✓ 1 teaspoon cayenne

- ✓ 1 teaspoon garlic

- ✓ 1 teaspoon chili powder

- ✓ 1 teaspoon onion powder

- ✓ 4 tablespoons salt

Directions:

1. Cut the meat into 1/4 inch thick strips and trim all the fat.

2. Mix all the ingredients into a marinade.

3. Soak the meat in the marinade for one hour.

4. Dehydrate at 155 degrees for a minimum of 10 hours.

Buffalo Jerky Recipe

Ingredients:

- ✓ 2 pounds buffalo meat

- ✓ 1/4 cup honey

- ✓ 1/2 cup soy sauce

- ✓ 1 tablespoon grated ginger

- ✓ 1 1/2 tablespoons red pepper flakes

✓ 5 minced garlic cloves

Directions:

1. Cut the meat into 1/4 inch thick strips and trim all the fat.

2. Mix the ingredients and marinate the meat overnight.

3. Dry in a dehydrator or on the lowest temperature in the oven with the door slightly open for ventilation.

Chicken Jerky Recipe

Ingredients:

✓ 2 pounds chicken meat

✓ 6 tablespoons salt

✓ 1/4 teaspoon pepper

✓ 1 teaspoon garlic powder

- ✓ 1 teaspoon salt per pound of meat

- ✓ 1 teaspoon onion powder

- ✓ 6 ounces molasses

- ✓ 6 ounces soy sauce

- ✓ 6 ounces teriyaki sauce

Directions:

1. Make the marinade and allow to sit while cutting your meat into 1/4 inch thick strips.

2. Add the strips to the marinade.

3. Top with water until you completely submerge the marinade.

4. Cover and refrigerate for a minimum of ten hours, but no more than sixteen hours.

5. Dry in the oven at 170 degrees for five hours, turning the meat halfway through.

Duck Jerky Recipe

Ingredients:

- ✓ 1 pound duck meat

- ✓ Lemon juice

- ✓ Dash of cumin

- ✓ Dash of Lowery's

- ✓ 2 tablespoons pepper

- ✓ 2 tablespoons meat tenderizer

- ✓ 2 tablespoons curing salt

- ✓ 2 tablespoons Worcestershire sauce

Directions:

1. Freeze the meat for about a half hour then cut into 1/4 inch thick strips.

2. Cure the meat while preheating the oven to 200 degrees.

3. Use the ingredients to evenly coat each strip by rubbing it into the meat.

4. Marinate in the fridge for a couple of hours.

5. Line a cookie sheet with foil and lay out the meat.

6. Dry for 2 to 8 hours, flipping once and having the door propped open for ventilation.

Elk Jerky Recipe

Ingredients:

- ✓ 1 chopped onion

- ✓ 1/3 cup Worcestershire sauce

- ✓ 5 teaspoons ground black pepper

- ✓ 5 teaspoons salt

Directions:

1. Cut meat into 1/4 inch thick strips.

2. Combine all ingredients.

3. Marinate strips for 12 to 24 hours and cover in the fridge.

4. Dry in the over at 125 to 135 degrees for six to ten hours with the door propped open.

Fish Jerky Recipe

Ingredients:

✓ Choice of fish

✓ 3/4 cup salt

✓ 1 1/2 quart water

✓ Curing salt

Directions:

1. Slice the fish into strips.

2. Marinate and cure for an hour.

3. Dry in a dehydrator or on top of foil in the oven at the lowest temperature.

Lamb Jerky Recipe

Ingredients;

- ✓ 1 pound lamb

- ✓ 1 tablespoon onion salt

- ✓ 2 tablespoons liquid smoke

- ✓ 4 tablespoons soy sauce

- ✓ 1/3 cup Worcestershire sauce

- ✓ 1 1/2 teaspoons seasoning hickory liquid

- ✓ 5 drops Tabasco sauce

Directions:

1. Cut meat into 1/4 inch thick strips and remove all fat.

2. Combine ingredients and let sit in the fridge, covered, marinating for 8 to 10 hours.

3. Dehydrator in the dehydrator at the lowest temperature for 12 to 24 hours.

Turkey Jerky Recipe

Ingredients:

- ✓ 1 tablespoon liquid smoke

- ✓ 4 tablespoons sugar

- ✓ 1/2 cup soy sauce

- ✓ 2 teaspoons of grated ginger

- ✓ 1 clove of garlic minced

- ✓ 2 pounds of turkey meat

Directions:

1. Mix the marinade and coat each piece of 1/4 inch thick turkey meat.

2. Allow to sit for six to twelve hours covered in the refrigerator.

3. Dehydrate in a dehydrator, flipping once.

Venison Jerky Recipe

Ingredients:

✓ 10 ounces soy sauce

✓ 1 cup brown sugar

✓ 1 cup burgundy wine

✓ 1/2 teaspoon garlic powder

✓ 1/2 teaspoon cayenne pepper

✓ 1/2 teaspoon onion powder

✓ 1 teaspoon salt

✓ 1 teaspoon pepper

✓ 2 teaspoons liquid smoke

Directions:

1. Cut meat into 1/4 inch thick strips.

2. Make the marinade, coat meat and cover before placing in refrigerator.

3. Smoke meat based on your preference.

Made in the USA
Las Vegas, NV
24 October 2024

10396545R00148